TO THE BARRICADES
The Anarchist Life of
Emma Goldman

Women of America
Milton Meltzer, Editor

SEA AND EARTH
The Life of Rachel Carson
By Philip Sterling

TONGUE OF FLAME
The Life of Lydia Maria Child
By Milton Meltzer

TO THE BARRICADES
The Anarchist Life of Emma Goldman
By Alix Shulman

LABOR'S DEFIANT LADY
The Story of Mother Jones
By Irving Werstein

QUEEN OF POPULISTS
The Story of Mary Elizabeth Lease
By Richard Stiller

PROBING THE UNKNOWN
The Story of Dr. Florence Sabin
By Mary Kay Phelan

MARGARET SANGER
Pioneer of Birth Control
By Lawrence Lader and Milton Meltzer

SOMEBODY'S ANGEL CHILD
The Story of Bessie Smith
By Carman Moore

THE SENATOR FROM MAINE
Margaret Chase Smith
By Alice Fleming

NEIGHBOR TO THE WORLD
The Story of Lillian Wald
By Irvin Block

TO THE BARRICADES

The Anarchist Life of Emma Goldman

by Alix Shulman

illustrated with photographs

Thomas Y. Crowell Company • New York

DESIGNED BY CAROLE FERN HALPERT

Manufactured in the United States of America

L. C. Card 72-132302
ISBN 0-690-83280-X

1 2 3 4 5 6 7 8 9 10

Quotations from *Living My Life*, by Emma Goldman, copyright 1931 by Alfred A. Knopf, Inc. Passage from Proudhon, as it appears in English translation in James Joll's *The Anarchists*, reprinted by permission of Little, Brown and Company.

To Polly

Preface

Though nowadays few people have heard of Emma Goldman, in her day she was known as "the most dangerous woman in the world." Small children were told, "If you're not good, Emma Goldman will get you." All she had to do was show up in a city or town and she was likely to be arrested—sometimes, as the police told her, "just because you're Emma Goldman." She was considered such a menace that finally the United States Government took away her citizenship and deported her.

Why did this "one little woman" strike such terror into the hearts of citizens, police forces, governments? Because Emma Goldman was an anarchist and a revolutionary. Jailed for conspiracy, for inciting to riot, for advertising birth control, for obstructing the draft, she dared to attack every authority that tried to put fences around the human spirit and make people go on "doing the things they hate to do, living the lives they loathe to live." No matter what the authorities did to her, nothing could stop her from fighting for a revolution to change all this, up until the day she died.

Now, in the 1970's, new generations of radicals are taking up Emma Goldman's fight. Like her, they are willing to face jail, exile, and even death because they believe that the world must be made over according to a new vision.

Emma Goldman's ideals and spirit are now very much alive. It is time that her story was heard again.

Contents

1 / Off to a Bad Start 1

2 / Cinderemma 12

3 / St. Petersburg 21

4 / Black Friday 34

5 / What is Anarchism? 49

6 / A Radical Life 64

7 / Homestead: The Supreme Deed 77

8 / Trials and Tribulations 90

9 / School Behind Bars 99

10 / Into the World 104

11 / Superwitch 118

12 / A Home for Lost Dogs 130

13 / The Red Queen and the Hobo King 144

14 / The Woman Question 158

15 / Conspiracy for Peace 174

16 / Red Scare 188

17 / Russia: A Dream Betrayed 203

18 / Exile 214

19 / Spain: A Dream Destroyed 224

20 / A Fitting End 234

Selected Bibliography 236

Index 240

Acknowledgments

I would like to thank the staff of New York University's Tamiment Library for making available to me the writings and documents of Emma Goldman's *Mother Earth* group, and the staff of the New York Public Library for helping me through the fine collections of *Emma Goldman Papers* and *Paul Orleneff Papers*. None of the conversations in To THE BARRICADES are invented; all are taken from contemporary writings.

I am indebted to Richard Drinnon, not only for his pioneer research on Emma Goldman, but for his helpful suggestions and careful reading of my manuscript. Discussions with my sisters in the women's liberation movement helped me formulate my ideas about anarchism and feminism; I am particularly grateful to Su Negrin and Gerry Levy for their criticisms of the manuscript.

Finally, I want to thank Martin Shulman for his editorial assistance and for the photograph of Emma Goldman's Home for Lost Dogs at 210 East Thirteenth Street, New York City.

TO THE BARRICADES
The Anarchist Life of
Emma Goldman

1

Off to a Bad Start

Life is the biggest bargain; you get it for nothing.
—YIDDISH PROVERB

Emma Goldman's story begins just over a hundred years ago and many thousands of miles away in the country of Russia. In those days Russia seemed to be a storybook land, with its onion-shaped steeples on village churches and its deep, snowy forests of birch and pine. But in reality the life was harsh and the people were often cruel. There, in 1869, Emma Goldman was born with four curses. She was born Russian, Jewish, female, and unloved.

The very first thing Emma learned when she was old enough to talk and understand was that she had not been wanted. Her father never tired of telling her how disappointed he was that she had been born a girl. "You can't be *my* child," he would tease her. "You don't look like me or your mother; you don't act like us!" Dark-haired and dark-eyed, Abraham Goldman wondered where Emma had got her blue eyes and blonde hair, so unusual in a Jewish child. "They must have come," he said, "from the pig's market," where Jews were not permitted to go because their religion forbids them to eat pork. The pig lady had cheated him, he would tell Emma with a bitter laugh, by giving him a girl-child instead of a boy.

Abraham Goldman had reason to be bitter; there was no sweetness in his life. Even his beautiful young wife Taube, whom he had married a year before Emma was born, had no love for him. She had loved a man only once, the young man she had married when she was fifteen. But he had fallen ill and died. When her first husband died, leaving her two small daughters, Lena and Helena, Taube buried with him all the love she would ever feel for a man. When she was barely out of mourning, her family arranged for her to marry Abraham Goldman. Like any good daughter in those times, she married the man her family selected for her, even though she did not love him. Marriage was a practical matter. And a widow with two small children, even a young and beautiful widow like Taube, was lucky to get any husband at all. But the loveless Goldman match was bad from the start.

Taube's first husband had left a little money when he died which Taube brought as a dowry to her new marriage. Abraham promptly invested it in a business. Almost immediately the business failed. When Taube became pregnant, the family had nothing to live on, and Emma's birth on June 27, 1869, was more of a curse than a blessing.

For most people in those days life in Russia was painfully hard. A handful of rich nobles owned all the land. Their huge estates were tended by great masses of poor, illiterate peasants called serfs. Until 1861, when a law was passed setting them free, these serfs had been owned as slaves by the nobles. After 1861 they could no longer be bought and sold or legally flogged, but otherwise they were hardly better off than slaves. While the nobles led fancy lives in their fine city houses in the winters and on their great country estates in the summers, the peasants led a wretched existence. They huddled together the year round in their crude huts, living on the ancient diet of black bread and tea. Into the short summers they tried to cram the backbreaking work of an entire year.

The kings of Russia, the czars, had ruled as tyrants for many centuries. The czar's every whim became law. His laws were carried out by a huge, cumbersome network of corrupt local officials. These bureaucrats grew fat filling their pockets with bribes. Everyone, even the poorest peasant, had to pay.

Bad as life was for most Russians, it was even more miserable for the Russian Jews. In the province of Kovno, where Emma was born, and in the surrounding provinces, lived great numbers of Jews. These solemn, religious people, darker in hair and skin than the Rus-

sians around them, had clung together as a separate people for many generations. Long hated by Christians,
even those Jews who were not religious had kept their
own Yiddish language, their own style of dress, and
their own ancient customs. As a group apart, they were
despised by almost everyone in Russia. As long as there
were few Jews in Russia, they managed to live unobtru-
sively. But when the land around Kovno with its large
Jewish population was conquered for the czar about seventy years before Emma was born, the Jews became a
special problem.

Seeing no easy way to get rid of the Jews, the czars issued special laws to keep them separate from other Russians. Jews could live only in certain provinces, then
only in certain towns. For a while all rural villages were
closed to them. In the towns and the cities they were
often herded into special streets and sections called
ghettos, which were sometimes walled off and locked at
night.

Even in the few places where Jews could live, they
were never left in peace. By law they could do only certain kinds of work, which kept them poor. Out of the
meager livings they managed to earn, they had to pay
special Jewish taxes to the czar and extra bribes to the
officials. There were laws restricting whom they could
hire, how they could dress, when and where they could
travel, where they could build their synagogues, and
even when they could marry. Life was so unsettled in
the ghettos, and Jews were so hemmed in by rules, that
it was all they could do just to survive.

Then, during Emma's childhood, something happened to threaten even their survival. A wave of pogroms broke out, terrorizing every Jewish heart in Russia. Originally *pogrom* meant "riot" in Russian. But after a while it came to mean a bloody attack on a community of Jews. In the middle of the day or night, without warning or reason, a band of armed, mounted raiders would ride down on a Jewish village to loot and murder. As soon as the horses were spotted in the distance, the cry would go through the streets and from house to house, "pogrom! pogrom!" and the defenseless Jews would hide until the raid was over. In tall boots and fur hats, waving swords high over their heads, the furious Cossacks would gallop into a ghetto, taking everything in sight. No Jew was safe, child or adult, woman or man. To a Russian raider, a Jew was not really a person—a Jew was simply a Jew, as a dog was a dog. No one ever knew how the pogroms were started. Some said they were ordered by the czar himself to take the minds of the Russian people off their misery.

Not long after Emma was born, the penniless Goldman family moved from Kovno Province to a tiny Russian village in the province of Kurland, near the Russian-German border. There, in the vast snow-covered region of noble estates worked by the peasants, Abraham Goldman managed to get a job as an innkeeper. Innkeeping was one of the few occupations open to Jews in the world outside the ghettos.

The little village of Popelan was hardly more than a stopping place on the lonely road between several larger provincial towns. The inn was its chief attraction. Surrounded by miles of unbroken farmland, Popelan was peopled by hardworking Russian peasants and run mainly by German-speaking officials. These officials, though Russian citizens, felt superior for their German ways. It would have been hard to say who hated the Jews more, peasants or officials.

The inn where Emma's life unfolded was a rough, cavernous barn. The official stop for the government stagecoaches, it was often crowded with travelers. The samovar on the great corner stove was always ready with quantities of hot tea. During the cold and terrible Russian winters, steam-breathing horses would pull sledges over the snowy fields up to the inn. Then the peasants with no place better to go, and the officials passing through the province on business, would spend the cold nights drinking Russian vodka before the fire, telling each other stories, and getting drunk. During the summer, when the meadows were green and the fields of grain grew high and golden, at the end of a long exhausting day the inn was the place where tired peasants came to relax. There they exchanged their gossip and learned the news of travelers from elsewhere in the province.

Often as not, as the evenings wore on and everyone grew drunk, someone would pass an insult or pick a quarrel. Then, before anyone could prevent it, the glasses and the fists would start to fly and the night would end in chaos. Some seasons hardly a night passed without a brawl. The children never knew what to expect. When Abraham tried to calm the guests, the peasants would ridicule him and the officials would hurl insults at him, because he was a Jew. It was all he could do just to run the inn and bear up under the constant abuse.

Like many another harassed man, Abraham took out his own suffering on everyone around him. With the peasants who worked at the inn, and even with his family, he was harsh and short-tempered. Sometimes when things went especially badly for him he would scream at his wife and beat his children. But his worst tantrums he seemed to save for Emma.

One day when Emma was playing marbles with her sisters, Lena and Helena, she learned that it was not only her father who resented her. Her sister Lena, it seemed, hated her for her own reasons. Emma had been winning at marbles that day, though she was only six, and much younger than Lena. Suddenly Lena accused her of cheating.

"Just like your father! He cheated us too!" Lena began screaming. "Your father robbed us of the money our father left. I hate you!"

Emma sat silent and bewildered.

"I hate you! You are not my sister!" Lena raged, and she gave Emma a violent kick.

Hurt beyond words, Emma dissolved in a torrent of tears. She ran hysterically to her other sister, Helena. She had *not* been cheating, she cried. Whatever her father had done was not her fault. Yet she never doubted what Lena said about the money, and she thought she must have somehow, without knowing it, done Lena some dreadful wrong. Helena took Emma in her arms to comfort her, as she always did. But Emma was inconsolable. "I wish I were grown," she sobbed. "Then I could pay back the money." Never again could she look at Lena without feeling a pang of guilt.

Winters passed, and two more children were born to the Goldmans—boys at last. With a family of seven now, and all the inn's servants and meals to supervise, Taube was always overworked and depressed. She had no time for Emma. Soon Emma's older sisters were spending all their days helping Taube with the endless chores. Her little brothers, Herman and Morris, were taken care of by a German "nursemaid" from just over the border. And Emma, too young to work and too old to need watching, was left on her own much of the time.

Stagecoaches came and departed, and much vodka was consumed at the inn. The quarreling Emma saw at the inn was easily matched by the cruelty she saw out in the world. Dogs were kicked, horses were whipped, children and wives were thrashed, and grown men beat each other. One day Emma was playing in the woods of Popelan when she heard someone shrieking in pain. She looked around to see where the cry was coming from. Suddenly through the trees she saw a peasant man, stripped to the waist, being flogged by a band of police. It was a hideous sight. The peasant's back was streaked with blood as the police sent the lash whistling through the air again and again. They were using the traditional Russian "knout"—a lash of many leather thongs twisted together with metal wires on the end of a long stick. It was the usual weapon for beating peasants.

Everyone in Popelan knew that peasants were sometimes flogged. Even Emma, who was only seven, had heard about it. But knowing about it was one thing;

watching it was quite another. It was the worst thing
Emma had ever seen. She ran home to the inn and
threw herself sobbing onto her bed. The sound of the
knout and the poor man's screams blended into a grotesque music that filled her head and haunted her for
many nights. She would never forget it.

But there were happy times in Popelan too. Among
the peasants who worked around the inn Emma had
one special friend. He was the stableboy, Petrushka. In
winter, when the meadows turned into plains of ice and
snow, Petrushka would hitch a horse to a sleigh at evening and take the children for long, slippery sleigh-
rides. Tucked under blankets, their sleigh bells jin-
gling, they would fly across the fields of silver snow,
listening for the Russian wolves howling in the distance
and watching the stars overhead. That was what winter
was for! Afterward at home, they would gather around
the fire to stay warm. Then, if she had time, Taube
would give the children tea and pancakes and jam, and
set a glass of vodka before Petrushka. Sometimes Petrushka would let Emma warm her insides with a sip.

In the summer Petrushka took the cows and sheep to
pasture. Every day Emma would follow him. In the
meadows, where blue cornflowers grew among the long
green grasses, Petrushka played his shepherd's flute for
her, piping his sweet tunes straight into her heart. They
would chase each other across the fields. He would
throw Emma playfully into the air and catch her, over
and over. Sometimes he would let her ride home from
the fields on his broad shoulders. Soon Petrushka became the center of Emma's life. Her happiest days were

spent playing with him in the meadows and her happiest nights dreaming of him in her bed. Sometimes she even stole fruits and sweets from her mother's kitchen to give to him.

Then one day her father had an argument with Petrushka. Without warning, in one of his fits of temper, Abraham sent the boy away.

Emma was sick over losing him. For weeks and months she dreamed and thought of nothing but Petrushka. How cruel it was, she thought, that peasants could be sent away, or beaten with the knout, at the mere whim of someone who happened to be of a higher rank. Gentle Petrushka could easily be beaten like the peasant in the woods, simply because he was born a peasant. Just as a Jew could be stoned by children in the streets simply for being a Jew. Nothing could be done about it. Everyone knew it happened all the time.

Once Emma and Helena watched an officer in the inn lash a young soldier across the face till his cheek bled. The boy had been polishing the officer's boots, and must have said something the officer didn't like. Helena was so enraged that she leaped at the officer and began hitting him with her fists. The whole Goldman family was in danger of going to prison because of it. Luckily for all of them, a colonel who happened to like Abraham Goldman managed to get the charges against the family removed. But the picture in Emma's mind of the soldier's bloody face was not removed. There it lingered with the picture of the bleeding peasant, and the banished Petrushka, and Abraham's tantrums, and Lena's kick. It lingered with all the other images of wanton cruelty that were daily piling up before her eyes. The gentle look of Popelan was a lie. The peaceful sky over the green summer meadows and the white winter woods concealed a brutal life.

"Out of the misery and murk of their lives, the Russian people had learned to make sorrow a diversion, to play with it like a child's toy," wrote the great Russian novelist Maxim Gorky. "Through their tedious weekdays they made a carnival of grief. A fire is entertainment, and on a vacant face, a bruise becomes an adornment." Everywhere, just under the surface of Russian life, were such violence and caprice and cruelty that Emma would never forget them.

Eventually she stopped dreaming of Petrushka. She knew he would never return.

2

Cinderemma

*There is no school which teaches the meaning of
despotism so well as the everyday experience of
children.*

—SARAH PRESTON-LONGLEY

Abraham Goldman considered himself a good father.
He worked like a horse to keep his family fed. He laid
down strict rules to teach his children right from
wrong. He punished them promptly when they were dis-
obedient and disciplined them soundly when they mis-
behaved. If there were too many quarrels in the house,
or if the children sometimes got too wild, or if Taube
cried too often, it was not his fault, he felt. He couldn't
always be attending to family matters. He was a busy
man. He did sometimes lose his temper, he had to
admit, but that was only because everyone always pro-
voked him.

When Emma turned eight, Abraham felt it was his duty to send her off to school. She had lived among illiterate peasants long enough. *His* children deserved better. As German schools were supposed to be better than Russian ones, he arranged for Emma to go to school in the German city of Koenigsberg, where Taube's mother and sisters lived. Emma would stay with them.

Everything was arranged, and Abraham and Emma set out for the German border, where Emma's grandmother was to meet them. On the way, Abraham began, as usual, to lecture Emma. He would be paying forty rubles a month for her tuition and board, he said gravely. That was a big expense for the family; she had better make it worthwhile. Emma nodded and listened.

"Be a good girl, study hard, obey your teachers and your grandmother," he admonished her. "If you are good, there is nothing I won't do for you.

"But," he said, raising his finger and lowering his voice menacingly, "if you misbehave, if you disgrace me, if you don't do well in school, or if I hear *any* complaint about you"—here he began to shake his finger in Emma's face—"I shall come to Koenigsberg to thrash you one last time, and then I will never take you back home again!"

By the time they neared the border, Abraham had worked himself into such a rage that Emma, trembling with fear, vowed with all her will to be good. She had only one wish left in the world—to get away from her father.

When at last she saw her grandmother, she ran to her as though she were her fairy godmother.

Koenigsberg, meaning "king's-mountain," was a neat German city of medium size. Five thousand Jews lived there in Emma's time. A city of culture, with a university, an opera house, theaters, boulevards, cafés, and many schools, it was by far the grandest place Emma had ever been.

Her grandmother was very poor. She shared her cramped apartment of three rooms and a kitchen with two of Emma's aunts, and the husband of one of them. This uncle and Emma took an immediate dislike to one another. Almost as soon as Emma joined the household, the battle between them began, though Emma's grandmother managed to preserve the peace.

Before long, Emma started school. She made a few friends and did well enough at first. Then, after about a month, her grandmother had to leave town. Suddenly, everything changed.

No sooner had her grandmother gone, than Emma's uncle took over and the nightmare began. Forty rubles a month, he declared, was not even enough for Emma's food. Her tuition was a waste, he said, and withdrew her from school. Then he set her to work in the house to "earn her keep."

Her father's cruelty had been capricious. Her uncle's was worse: it was calculated. Day after day, from dawn until evening, Emma was forced like some poor Cinderella to fetch the food, make the beds, clean the house, scrub the floors, shine the boots, wash the clothes. Terrified of her uncle, she worked uncomplainingly all day long. When her shoes wore out, she worked in her rubbers. But no matter how much she did, her uncle was never satisfied. Soon he had her cooking the meals as well. Every month he sent word to Abraham that Emma was doing nicely in school. And every month he pocketed the forty rubles.

Remembering her father's dire threats, Emma was much too frightened to send word to her parents. At night she would cry herself to sleep and hope for her grandmother's return.

Her aunts were as afraid of her uncle as she was, and didn't dare to interfere. Only two spinster sisters who lived below them in the house were any comfort to Emma. Sometimes when her uncle was away, Emma would visit the sisters secretly. They would listen to her story and soothe her with toasted almonds, and flowers from their garden, and affection.

One day toward sundown, after she had worked steadily since dawn, Emma felt she could not do another chore without dropping. She told her uncle.

"Lazy!" he screamed. He slapped her across the face, then kicked her down a flight of stairs.

She lay dazed at the bottom of the stairs, her body bruised and her ankle sprained, until the two spinster sisters found her.

"The child is dead!" shouted one.

"The scoundrel has killed her!" screamed the other.

Gently they took Emma into their parlor and promised to protect her from her uncle. They plied her with all the toasted almonds she could eat. They called a doctor, and one of her aunts sent for her father.

Days later, Abraham Goldman arrived at the house. The sisters led him to his daughter.

Emma was terrified that he would be angry at her for getting into so much trouble. When she heard him approaching her, she froze in her bed.

Abraham looked at Emma without a word. Far from being angry, he was so alarmed by how wasted she looked that he took her in his arms and kissed her. It was the only kiss he had given her since she was four years old.

Abraham took his daughter back to snowy Popelan, but not for long. Before the winter was over he lost his position as innkeeper. The family, penniless once again, had nowhere to live.

Abraham hoped Taube's relatives might help them. He returned to Koenigsberg with the whole family. There was no money at all, but the Koenigsberg rabbi, a distant relative of Taube's, promised to get free schooling for the children.

Emma's second venture into school lasted longer than the first. This time she stayed three and a half years. Her father, unlike her uncle, took school very seriously. Once when Emma brought home a report card with a low mark for deportment, Abraham flew into such a rage that he began pounding her with his fists. When Helena tried to protect Emma, as she so often did, he beat Helena too. He kept on beating them until he fainted.

Other times he would flog Emma with a lash, or stand her in the corner for hours, or make her walk back and forth carrying a full glass of water under threat of whipping for each drop she spilled. Her father

treated Emma so savagely that she would always remember his cruelty as "the nightmare of my childhood." Still, she kept on trying to win his love. All her life she had been frightened of his fury, but it took years before her fear hardened into hatred. At first she tried to obey his wishes, whatever he asked. But his demands for obedience grew so strict and outrageous that eventually she realized it would be impossible to really please him. Not until then did she turn rebellious. But once the change began, it never stopped. She started taking pleasure in revolt. After that, the more Abraham demanded, the more contrary she became.

At school her teachers were cruel or, at best, indifferent. Under that harsh routine, the rebel in her grew. Two teachers she particularly hated and fought.

Her first enemy was the religious instructor. Given to whacking the children across the palms of their hands with a ruler, he was the terror of the school. Like the rest of her family, Emma had never been especially religious. Now, seeing how brutal this instructor was, she lost whatever respect for religious authority she might have had. She decided to take revenge on him, and organized the rest of the students to help her. They tied his coattails to the table; they slipped snails into his pockets; they stuck pins in the pillows of his chair. When he found out that Emma was behind the pranks, he hit her hands harder than the others'.

Emma's other enemy, the geography teacher, brutalized the children more slyly. Using his position of power, he made his female students stay after school and submit to his caresses. The girls were much too frightened to report him. One day Emma lost her temper and openly rebuffed him in class. He was furious. He made such a scene, clawing Emma's arm and shouting, that his secret came out in the open. After that he was fired.

In school there was one teacher, the German instructor, whom Emma loved dearly. This teacher was a patient and tender woman who took a special interest in Emma. She invited Emma to her house, where they read together her favorite German novels. She gave her extra lessons and took her to her first opera. She persuaded a friend to teach Emma French and music, and she shared with her pupil her own love of everything German. Under her teacher's affectionate care, Emma was soon devouring German literature and culture for herself with the passion she brought to everything she loved. She longed to know everything, and her teacher made everything seem possible to know. With the world suddenly opening before her, Emma decided to become a doctor. It would be hard for a girl, and harder for a Jew. Yet it was still possible. She would try, anyway.

Toward the end of her last year at primary school, Emma's father was called back to Russia to manage a cousin's dry-goods store in the Russian capital, St. Petersburg. Since Jews were not legally permitted to enter Russia, the family divided in half to make the dangerous border crossing. Abraham took Lena and Helena with him; Taube and the younger children were to follow later.

Emma didn't want to leave school or her German teacher. She begged her mother to let her stay behind at her grandmother's. She pleaded and pestered until she won. Her mother said she could stay on in Koenigsberg, but only on one condition. Emma must pass all the requirements for the *Gymnasium,* the academic high school.

At last, thought Emma, her future was in her own hands. She spent every moment she could preparing for the entrance exam for the *Gymnasium.*

Finally the day of the exam came. Emma took it and passed easily. Everything seemed to be coming together for her for the first time in her life.

Now there was only one last requirement. She had to get a character recommendation from her religious instructor—her old enemy who liked to strike the children's hands. Emma dreaded asking anything of him, but she had no choice. Her future depended on his signature. If she could get the letter, she would be admitted to the *Gymnasium.* Without the letter she would not. There were no exceptions.

Steeling herself, Emma reluctantly approached the hated teacher. Class was about to begin; all the students were in their seats. As calmly and politely as she could, Emma explained why she had come. She told him that she had passed the entrance exam for the *Gymnasium,* and now she needed a character recommendation from him. As she waited to hear his reply, she knew she was at his mercy.

Her teacher looked at her hard for one long, silent moment. Everyone in the class was listening. Then slowly he began to speak. He told Emma contemptuously what a terrible child she was. He said she would probably wind up being hanged as a public menace. "You have no respect for your elders," he shouted, "no respect for authority. I will *never* recommend your character! You have none!"

Emma turned slowly and left the room. She knew it was useless to fight. She had already been bullied and battered enough in her short life to know that people in a position of unchecked power have the final say. It had happened to Petrushka; now it was happening to her. Without her teacher's letter, her hopes for an academic education melted away like snowflakes. And there was not a single thing she could do.

Emma was twelve years old. She would have to leave Germany now and return with her family to St. Petersburg, where her father, who was fast becoming her enemy, awaited them.

3

St. Petersburg

No army can withstand the force of an idea whose time has come.

—Victor Hugo

It was still dark and bitter cold as the three youngest Goldmans and their mother approached the stream dividing Germany from Russia. They were going to St. Petersburg to join the rest of the family. Taube had put herself in the hands of border smugglers, who made a business of getting people across the frontier illegally. It was a risky business, but for Jews there was no other way. She had been warned by the border smugglers that she and the children would have to wade noiselessly across the half-frozen stream and through deep snowdrifts to reach the Russian side. They would have to get across before daybreak. Though the border guards had been duly bribed to let the family pass, the soldiers could never be trusted. Bribe or no, they might shoot at the Jews if they took too long crossing or attracted any attention. They might even decide to shoot at them for fun.

As she came up to the stream, Emma hesitated. She was already ill with the flu and half frozen from the cold. Now, seeing the icy stream in the dim moonlight, she began shivering with fright. The strange banks looked menacing. She wanted to turn back.

But ahead of her, her mother, loaded down with bundles, was already wading into the water, and there were soldiers all around them. There was no turning back. She must follow her mother quickly.

Bracing herself, Emma picked up her little brother and plunged ahead into the stream. Suddenly, as the icy water hit her, she felt a terrible stinging pain, like hot irons, all up and down her spine and her legs. The pain did not let up until they reached the other bank of the stream. Though her teeth were chattering now, and she was in a sweat, she could not stop moving. They were still in danger. She had to run and keep running; she had to stay close behind her mother.

They ran all the way to the nearest inn on the Russian side, sucking the cold air into their lungs. When at last they reached the inn, it was clear that Emma was very ill. She had a high fever, and she was weak and in pain. The women at the inn gave her hot tea to sip, and tucked her under a featherbed with hot bricks packed around her. But her fever didn't pass. Even after the long journey by stage from the border to St. Petersburg her legs were racked with pain.

At the time the four were traveling to St. Petersburg, the great Russian capital was in a state of terror. The czar's police were in control of the city. Less than a year before, on March 1, 1881, Czar Alexander II had been assassinated. Although the assassins belonged to a fairly small organization of revolutionary men and women, they were an extreme faction of a much larger movement against the czar's tyrannical government. This movement, called populism ("people-ism"), had been developing for decades. It included people of many different shades of political opinion. But all of them had at least this in common: they all believed that the terrible cruelties of Russian life could never be eliminated until the czarist government itself was eliminated. They all believed that the land, the factories, and the power to make decisions should be taken from the rich nobles and the czar and given to the Russian people themselves.

These were radical ideas. The word "radical" comes from the Latin word *radix,* which means "root." A radical is someone who tries to get to the very root of a problem, to the bottom of things, instead of changing things only at the surface. No mere "reformers," the populists were radicals.

The assassins of the czar had hoped that their act would touch off a widespread popular revolution against the czar. They had hoped that the Russian peasants, the workers in the cities, the students, and all the people who hated tyranny would rise up together and with one mighty blow overthrow the monstrous government. Then tyranny would melt away like the Russian snows in the spring, flooding the land with freedom.

Their plan had failed miserably. Not only was there no revolution, but the assassination of Alexander II had the very opposite effect. The new czar, Alexander III, vowed to crush all revolutionary activity and destroy all radical opinion of every kind. The new czar saw enemies everywhere. Even people who wanted no more change than for the czar to continue to rule, but under a constitution, fell under suspicion as enemies of the State. The czar's police rounded up most of the populist leaders, including those who had nothing to do with the assassination. These leaders were either killed, exiled, or imprisoned. Ideas, both written and spoken, were ruthlessly censored. Meetings were forbidden. No opinion escaped suspicion.

Usually, when a calamity occurred in Russia the Jews were held to blame. Now the Jews fell under suspicion for the assassination of the czar. The new czar issued a package of new, harsher laws against the Jews, and all over Russia systematic persecution of the Jews began. The worst wave of pogroms Russia had ever experienced broke out during the year Emma returned to Russia. The government officials, when they did anything at all about the pogroms, encouraged them. No Jew in Russia felt safe. Many victims of the massacres in the towns fled to the large ghettos of the great cities, hoping to find safety in the crowd.

By 1882 the St. Petersburg ghetto was a teeming, terrorized slum. If it was ordinarily crowded and unhealthy, it was doubly so now. It was packed to overflowing with refugees from the pogroms. With so many extra people trying to earn a living in the ghetto, jobs were very hard to get. Since people were willing to do almost anything to earn money for food, wages were extremely low. In fact, life was so hard in the ghetto that many Jews were packing up what few belongings they had, and fleeing from Russia altogether. Their goodbyes were filled with promises to send for their families when their fortunes were made. It was every Jew's hope to leave.

Emma's sister Lena was one of those who left. Like most of the others, she went to the United States, a young country known to welcome people from other lands.

The snows were already melting and the birches were beginning to push out their new green shoots when Emma and her family reached St. Petersburg in the early spring of 1882. Emma's back and legs still ached, and everyone was worn out from the journey. Still, they greeted the city smiling. Abraham had a good job at last. Emma would be with Helena again. If her mother kept her newest promise, Emma would soon enroll in a Russian school. And all of them could begin to enjoy the rare pleasures available in a great capital city like St. Petersburg.

They went straight to Abraham's cousin's store—only to find the store closed and Abraham once more out of a job. Lena was gone; only Helena was earning any money at all. Emma, though only twelve years old, would probably have to go to work herself, instead of starting school.

Just in time resourceful Taube convinced her brothers to lend Abraham some money. With it he opened a small grocery store of his own in the ghetto, and Emma entered school after all.

At school she began to study Russian literature as she had once studied German. Very soon she got caught up in the populist ideas that were everywhere in the charged air of the city and on the lips of her fellow students. The authorities had already begun to hunt down radicals, and had banned all books and journals that discussed the radical ideas of the populists. But the forbidden books were passed secretly from hand to hand, and the "new" ideas were discussed in small, secret meetings and whispered everywhere. However many arrests the police might make, they could not control the thoughts inside people's minds or destroy the dreams inside their heads. The simple and powerful ideas that thoughtful radicals had been spreading for more than twenty years could not be stamped out by order of the czar. In secret, people spoke of dividing up the land of the idle nobles among the peasants who worked it. They whispered the forbidden notion that people should rule themselves, instead of being ruled by nobles. They dared to imagine equality and a single rule of justice for everyone, instead of one kind of justice for nobles and another kind for the rest of the people. Above all, they longed for an end to the savage tyranny of the government. These ideas passed like sparks from mouth to ear, lighting little fires in people's minds. The populist dream continued to glow.

As Emma learned about the ideas of the revolutionaries, she became enchanted by their simple, compelling truths. Freedom, justice, equality—who could not love them?

In Germany, when she had first heard about the assassination of the czar, she had been baffled by the assassins' motives. Now, talking to the students and teachers of St. Petersburg, she began to understand them. She began to see why the assassins, who had been hanged for their act, were considered martyrs and heroes by many Russians, instead of common murderers. They had killed the czar in order, somehow, to rid Russia of a terrible, oppressive government. Like the knights of the fairy tales, they had wanted to slay the monster. They did not care that they would be caught and hanged. Willingly they sacrificed their own lives for the sake of all the Russians suffering under the curse of the czar. Their deed had been selfless. They had been guided by an enchanting vision of the future.

From one of her teachers Emma heard the story of young, revolutionary Vera Zasulich, who four years earlier had wounded the governor of St. Petersburg. The governor, the terrible General Trepov, was the terror of the city and the surrounding province. Everyone feared and hated him. He had his police flog peasants and students; he ordered people tortured, imprisoned, exiled, and even killed for their political opinions. When Vera Zasulich shot him, the people of St. Petersburg rejoiced, and overnight she became a popular hero. Even though she confessed to the shooting, she was acquitted at her trial.

Emma was moved by the story of this brave girl who was not afraid to sacrifice her life. Soon Emma, too, began to regard the revolutionaries and the assassins of the czar as heroes and martyrs.

After Emma had been in school about six months, it became clear that the family needed more money than the grocery store could bring. Now Emma would have to go to work. Six months of school was not very long, but it was long enough for Emma to inhale the radical ideas around her. When she left school, she took them with her.

The first job Emma got was knitting shawls at home. The pay was so low that sometimes she had to work all day long and into the night in order to earn a mere twelve rubles a month. When she was thirteen she gave up knitting for factory work. A cousin gave her a job in his glove factory, where six hundred girls and women worked in one large, stuffy, windowless room from early morning till night. The work was exhausting and the pay was low. But Emma, who had always had incredible energy, read and studied each night.

Once she had eagerly read German novels with her teacher in Koenigsberg. Now, in every spare moment, she devoured the forbidden Russian novels that Helena somehow managed to get hold of. It would take her two hours in the morning to get to work and two hours more to get home at night, traveling both ways in the dark. But late at night in her ghetto room she read the stories of free men and women working together to build a just society. Emma longed to breathe the free air that rose from the pages of those books. Why couldn't she, too, live only by her dreams? Soon she was taking nothing for granted. She suddenly saw that nothing in the world was God-given, nothing in society *had* to be the way it was. People made society; people could change it. She began to question everything. The more she read the more dissatisfied she became with her restricted, conventional ghetto life. Though she had had to quit school, her real education was only beginning.

Abraham couldn't understand Emma's wild new ideas. How rebellious his daughter was growing! He wished she were docile and obedient like ordinary girls; but with her fair skin and golden hair she was nothing like most daughters of the ghetto. She was small and quick like a rabbit, with the will and spirit of a wild colt. Each day she became harder and harder to manage. He knew only one way to deal with her—stricter rules, louder no's, harder beatings.

At fifteen Emma went to work in a corset factory. There she made a number of friends her father knew nothing about. Mostly they were girls she worked with, and some young men they sometimes met after work. But if Emma joined her friends after work, she would have to invent stories to explain why she was late getting home.

Once, when Emma and her friends had stopped in the Summer Garden after work, her father chanced to see them. From his hiding place Abraham watched the girls and boys talking and laughing together. He grew angrier by the second. Then he hurried home to wait for Emma.

Emma walked in a little later and gave some ordinary excuse for being late. Abraham exploded. Losing all control, he threw Emma violently against the shelves of the grocery store. Jars of preserves flew in every direction. "I will not have a loose daughter!" he screamed, pounding her with his fists.

Emma knew that what she had done was not so terrible. Why did her father hate her so? It was no use trying to get along with him. She would have to deceive him instead, until the day she could escape from him for good.

After that, fooling Abraham gave Emma some of her happiest times. Her finest triumph came when Helena's boss invited Helena and Emma to a dance.

Emma was thrilled to be invited. She had never been to a dance, and this one was the annual ball given by the fashionable German Club. The trouble was that Abraham was sure to forbid Emma to go with Helena. The girls didn't even dare ask him.

Then they hit on a plan. If they could make a gown for Emma in time for the dance, Abraham would have to let her go. Poor as they were, it would be too wasteful for him to refuse. Helena bought some fabric out of her own salary. The girls worked on the gown secretly night after night until it was finished.

At last, picking her words carefully, Helena asked Abraham to let Emma go to the dance. Miraculously, Abraham said yes.

Emma was wild with excitement when, after agonies of waiting, the day of the dance arrived. It would be her first ball, her first long dress. She almost managed to get through the day when suddenly, at the last moment, for some trivial reason, Abraham decided that Emma couldn't go after all. She had committed some offense, and for punishment, he said, she would stay home and learn her lesson.

Beside herself with rage and disappointment, Emma swore to go to the dance no matter what. "I'll stay home with you," offered Helena, but Emma ignored her. If necessary, she told her sister, she would run away from home.

Emma waited until her parents were asleep. Then, quietly, she put on her gown, arranged her yellow hair, and woke Helena. When both girls were dressed they tiptoed to the door and slipped out of the house.

The ball was like something out of a fairy tale. Emma was asked for every single dance. Whatever might be in store for her at home the next day, it would surely be worth it, she thought. As the night wore on she told Helena breathlessly that she would be happy to *die* dancing.

The sisters danced until just before dawn; then they ran home. As they stole into the house only moments ahead of the day, everything was still. Their parents were sound asleep. Quietly the girls slipped into bed and instantly fell asleep themselves. Abraham never even suspected how his daughters had fooled him.

Emma might have gone on that way—working in the day, reading in her free time, and deceiving her father at night—if Abraham hadn't decided later that year to marry her off. It was an easy way to get rid of a troublesome daughter. Jewish marriages were almost always arranged by the parents, and though Emma was young, fifteen was not too young. Hadn't Emma's own mother first been married at fifteen? Abraham set about bargaining for a husband for his blue-eyed daughter, and in due time he announced his plan to her.

Emma was frantic. She had seen enough loveless marriages to know she would marry only for love. She was ready to do anything in the world to escape Abraham's newest trap. She wanted to study, she wanted to travel, she wanted to know life before giving up her freedom to a man. She begged her father not to make her marry; she pleaded with him to let her continue studying.

Furious at being opposed, Abraham grabbed Emma's French grammar book and hurled it into the fire. "Girls do not have to learn much!" he screamed at her. "All a Jewish daughter needs to know is how to prepare minced fish, cut noodles fine, and give the man plenty of children!"

Now Emma was in real danger. If her father insisted, she would have to marry. Girls had no rights. And Helena, her only ally, was getting ready to join Lena in America. Emma begged Helena to take her along. It was the only certain way to be free. But Abraham wouldn't hear of it. He had his own plans for Emma.

Helena offered to pay Emma's fare, and Emma pleaded and wept and used every argument she could think of. Still, Abraham held firm. Finally, when nothing else would soften him, Emma told her father she would drown herself in the river if he didn't let her go.

Emma's preferences had always been such a mystery to Abraham that he had to take her threat seriously. He had no idea what his impetuous, stubborn, headstrong daughter might do. She had such an indomitable will that she might actually drown herself, he feared, simply because she had threatened to. Reluctantly he consented to let her go.

After that Emma could do nothing but dream and plan and prepare for America until it was time to leave. She had heard so much about the marvelous golden land where everyone was equal and free.

At the end of December, 1882, she left St. Petersburg with Helena and twenty-five rubles that her father had grudgingly given her for the trip. Later she would miss St. Petersburg, and the friends and books and music she was leaving behind. But now she felt no regrets. On the German steamship *Elbe,* bound for the United States, she was wild with excitement. She and Helena were traveling "steerage" with hundreds of other passengers all herded together like cattle in tiny quarters. But to Emma it felt like freedom, compared to the stifling home she was leaving behind. At last she was living with someone for whom she felt nothing but love. Her future was open and free.

She watched the endless expanse of ocean and counted the days.

4

Black Friday

Give me your tired, your poor,
Your huddled masses yearning to breathe free,
The wretched refuse of your teeming shore,
Send these, the homeless tempest-tossed to me:
I lift my lamp beside the golden door.
—EMMA LAZARUS, INSCRIPTION FOR THE STATUE OF
LIBERTY

The deck was crowded with excited, eager people, all straining to glimpse the new land looming through the fog. Emma and Helena clung to each other, their eyes overflowing with tears. At long last they had reached America. The Statue of Liberty, erected that very year in New York harbor, emerged through the mist to welcome them.

As soon as they left the ship, their expectations received a sudden jolt. Instead of the promised welcome, they were greeted with hostility or indifference. The first Americans they met, the government immigration officials, ordered and shoved the immigrants around as though they were so many boxes of cheap merchandise. Almost from the moment they landed in New York, it seemed to Emma and Helena that life—at least for the poor—would not be a great deal different in America from what it had been in Russia.

The sisters made their way to Rochester, New York, where Lena had prepared a room in her house for them to share. They soon discovered that most of the Jews of Rochester, like the Jews of Russia, lived together in one section of the city where English was hardly ever spoken. True, there was no law forcing them into the ghetto here as there was in Russia. And some Jews, they heard, had grown rich and moved away. But to Emma and Helena the effect was sadly the same. The immigrants seemed locked out of American life by their foreign ways, their inability to speak English, and their poverty. People were expected to conform to American ways; those who didn't were feared or despised. Too often people who couldn't speak English, and even those who spoke it with heavy accents, were thought stupid, just as those who couldn't get jobs were thought lazy. Even those immigrants who became American citizens were often treated as second-class citizens, chiefly because of their language.

Lena and her husband, like most of the Russian immigrants, were almost as poor in America as they had been in Russia. Though Lena, expecting her first child, tried to make her sisters feel welcome, Emma and Helena knew they were a burden to her. The girls took the first jobs they could find so that they could begin to pay for their board. Helena got a job retouching photographs. Emma went to work in a factory making overcoats.

Like so many of her first experiences in America, the first factory job Emma took was a disappointment and a lesson. The Garson clothing factory in Rochester was known as a model factory. There was plenty of room to work in, and there was fresh air to breathe. Then why was working here so much harder than it had been at the glove factory in St. Petersburg? In St. Petersburg hundreds of workers had been squeezed together in one dark, stuffy room. They had worked long hours and had been poorly paid. But they had not had to work under pressure. They had been allowed to sing and talk to each other and even to take two extra breaks a day for tea. They had been treated like people, not machines. Here in America in Garson's model clothing factory no one was allowed to sing or talk or even go to the bathroom without the foreman's permission. The only break in the long day was a half hour for lunch, and the rest of the time the foreman watched them closely to see that they worked their very hardest.

Once a friend of Emma's fainted on the job from overwork. When Emma and a few other workers rushed to her aid, the foreman shouted, "Back to your machines! What do you mean stopping work now? Do you want to be fired?"

Impetuous as ever, Emma stormed out of the factory with her sick friend, cursing the foreman as she went. "You can deduct the time from my pay," she threw back at him hotly. The next day, needing the money, both girls were dutifully back at their machines.

Despite her unusual stamina, Emma found her job utterly exhausting. She was so driven at work that by the time she returned home each night she could do nothing but collapse into bed. For doing this hard and demoralizing work ten and a half hours a day, she received a salary of $2.50 a week. It was hardly enough to pay Lena for her keep, let alone to buy anything for herself. She longed to be able to buy a book now and then, or a bouquet of flowers. Everyone, she felt, deserved some beauty and joy in life—not just work and exhaustion and more work.

After Lena's baby was born and the household expenses went up, Emma realized she would have to ask for a raise. The owner of the factory, Mr. Garson, was known in Rochester as a generous and charitable man. He was even the chairman of the United Jewish Charities of Rochester. Emma decided to go directly to him for her raise.

She was ushered into Mr. Garson's elegant office. Mr. Garson smiled at her as he puffed on a cigar, but he did not ask her to sit down. On a table Emma saw a vase full of American Beauty roses. She had seen such roses before, in a flower shop, and had thought them so lovely that she had gone into the shop to ask the price. Two roses, she had been told, cost $3.00—more than her entire weekly salary! Now she stared at the mass of roses on the table in a kind of daze.

"Well, what can I do for you?" asked Mr. Garson at

last. Emma shook her mind free of the roses and told Mr. Garson in faltering English that she had come to ask for a raise. She explained that after paying her board and carfare she didn't have enough left over from her salary to buy even an occasional twenty-five-cent book or theater ticket.

"You have rather extravagant tastes for a factory girl," said Mr. Garson. He puffed on his cigar. He explained that if he gave Emma a raise he would have to raise the other workers' wages too. "I can't afford that," he said.

Years later, in 1913, the immigrant women who worked in the textile mills of Lawrence, Massachusetts, went on strike. Demanding not only higher wages but decent human treatment, they marched behind banners that read, "We want bread and roses too." The militant women of Lawrence, with many radicals (including Emma) behind them, eventually won their strike. But in Rochester in 1886, alone against Mr. Garson, Emma lost. With barely enough money for bread and nothing at all for roses, she quit her job the next day.

The American dream was fast turning into a nightmare. Almost everyone Emma knew was poor and exploited. Worse, no one seemed to expect a better future. America welcomed foreigners chiefly, it seemed, as a source of cheap labor. Everyone talked endlessly about making money, but everyone seemed stuck in poverty. American "equality" was apparently little more than a myth. It turned out that there was a hierarchy in America, a pecking order, as there had been in Russia—as perhaps there was everywhere. All over America whites exploited the despised blacks. In Rochester native

Americans used and despised all the foreign immigrants. German-speaking Jews like Mr. Garson exploited the poorer Russian-speaking Jews. Emma found
most of the people she met, with their gossip and their
chatter about money, dull and grating. No one she
knew seemed ever to have been touched, as she had
been, by a vision of a better society. No one seemed to
care about anything but getting ahead. With almost no
one to talk to, Emma longed for the friends and excit-
ing Russian conversation she had left behind in St. Petersburg.

When she discovered a local German socialist club,
she began to attend its meetings. Its dream of society
was something like the dream of the Russian populists
Emma had known in Russia. Both hated the existing
system and believed it could be changed. These socialists, however, knew more precisely how they wanted to
change it. They wanted to replace the present government, run by property owners, with a government run
by and for workers. The socialist government would see
to it that everyone helped produce the necessities of life,
and that everyone received a fair share. It was a good
plan, Emma thought, but she was not inspired by these
German socialists as she had been by the Russian radicals. Small, dreary Rochester was nothing like St. Petersburg, where the very air had been charged with radical ideas. In America the centers of radicalism were far
from Rochester, in large cities like New York and Chicago. It was in those cities that the struggling American
labor movement was making headway. The German socialists of Rochester were few and weak and isolated;

they were not the fiery, dedicated students Emma had known in Russia. Between meetings, and sometimes even during them, Emma was bored and lonely.

Soon after she quit her first job she found another, better job. She was paid a little more and driven a little less. Working at the machine next to hers was a young man named Jacob Kershner. Like Emma, Jacob was a Russian-Jewish immigrant, and like Emma, he felt lonely and lost in hostile, English-speaking America. Though he had immigrated years ago, he had made almost no friends. Both desperate for Russian conversation, Emma and Jacob soon began walking to work together every day. Jacob lent Emma his Russian books to read. They spent their time talking for hours in Russian and even going to dances together.

Late in the fall of 1886, Emma's parents and brothers arrived in America. Russia had finally become unbearable for them as Jews. Emma and Helena left Lena's house to prepare a home for their parents. Eventually they took Jacob in to live with them as a boarder. And before long, he asked Emma to marry him.

Emma didn't know what to do. She was fond of Jacob, and she needed his company, but she had been resisting marriage since she was fifteen. The main reason she had left Russia was to escape her father's efforts to marry her off. She had always wanted to be independent. Now, at eighteen, still longing to be independent, she was terribly discouraged. She had traveled halfway around the world, it seemed, in search of freedom, only to find herself in many ways more lonely, more restricted, and more dependent than ever. Marrying would at least cure her loneliness. It would end her parents' hold on her. It would at least be a change—perhaps, she thought, a change for the better. Her parents, Lena, and all their friends urged her to marry. Only Helena, who had disliked Jacob from the start, was cool to the idea.

In February 1887 Emma and Jacob were married by a local rabbi. Her family rejoiced that their wild, headstrong daughter would at last be tamed.

Instead of solving her old problems, Emma's marriage only created new ones. Because it was disgraceful for a married woman to work away from home, Emma had to give up her job. With it, she gave up what little financial independence she might have had. Instead of curing her loneliness, her marriage only increased it. Jacob was away at work all day long, and soon he began staying out to play cards every night. Sometimes, when he came home, he would have a jealous tantrum, accusing Emma of being unfaithful with everyone around. The newlyweds began to hate each other.

Fortunately there were other things for Emma to think about besides her unhappy marriage. Some time before, a series of events known as the Haymarket Affair had captured her interest. It had started with a bomb and culminated in a trial of eight men. Now, with her marriage falling apart, she grew more and more absorbed in the outcome of the Haymarket Affair. She would bury herself in the newspapers each night. With difficulty she would translate from English, word by word, the fearful story of the Haymarket trial.

In Chicago, back in May 1886, about forty thousand

men, many of them immigrants, had been on strike for a shorter workday, the "eight-hour day." Chicago was alive with meetings and speeches and rallies to help the strike. It was also alive with police and Pinkerton detectives perfectly willing to crush the strike for the sake of keeping "order." A number of the strike leaders belonged to a revolutionary group who called themselves anarchists. In many ways their ideals were similar to those of the populists and socialists Emma was attracted to.

On May 3 the police had tried to quell a fight between strikers and strikebreakers at a large Chicago factory by firing on the strikers. They had injured several men and killed one. The following night a mass rally was called to protest the police attack. The demonstration was to be held in the Haymarket, a large open square in the heart of Chicago.

The rally proceeded peacefully. The anarchist leaders delivered angry speeches, but none called for violence. The mayor of Chicago, who had gone to the rally to observe, left toward the end of the evening because it was so orderly. He stopped by the police station to tell the captain on duty that he was sure there would be no trouble, and he went home to bed.

Just before the rally was to break up, as the last speech was ending, the captain with a force of 180 police walked into the rally and unaccountably ordered everyone to leave. All of a sudden a dynamite bomb exploded in the midst of the police. It had been thrown from somewhere near the speakers' platform. One policeman died instantly and almost seventy others were injured, six of them fatally. Within seconds the police opened fire on the crowd in response, and everyone who could get away fled.

No one ever discovered who threw the bomb, but immediately it was labeled an "anarchist plot." The most prominent Chicago anarchists were arrested and charged with conspiracy to murder. In all, eight men were indicted.

First Chicago, then the entire nation, succumbed to hysteria, demanding vengeance against the anarchists. No one bothered to wait until they had been tried. Newspapers all across the country clamored for anarchist blood. Even the sober *Albany Law Journal* declared:

> It is a serious thought that the lives of good and brave men . . . should be, even for one hour, in a great city, at the mercy of a few long-haired wild-eyed, bad-smelling, atheistic, reckless foreign wretches, who never did an honest hour's work in their lives. . . . We hope they will be . . . extirpated from the face of the earth.

A campaign of terror began against anarchists and radicals everywhere. It made a fair trial for the accused men practically impossible.

When the trial began in June 1886, everyone seemed to know what the outcome would be. Even the judge seemed to have decided in advance that the anarchists were guilty. There was hardly any evidence offered against them except to show that they were anarchists. They were being tried for their political opinions, not for throwing the bomb. Their trial was so unfair that years later the governor of Illinois pardoned those of the prisoners who were still living at the time. But by then most of them were dead, convicted by a biased court.

At the end of the trial the prosecutor asked the jury to impose the death sentence on the anarchists. He said:

> Law is upon trial. Anarchy is on trial. These men have been selected, picked out by the grand jury and indicted because they were leaders. They are no more guilty than the thousands who follow them. Gentlemen of the jury: convict these men, make examples of them; hang them and you save our institutions, our society.

All eight men were found guilty. One was sentenced to fifteen years in prison, and seven were sentenced to death.

Emma had first heard about the case through the Rochester papers. Like most newspapers, they were ardently against the anarchists. But one Sunday night at a socialist meeting she heard a speech defending the condemned men. All through the meeting, police armed with clubs lined the auditorium.

Emma was strangely moved by the defense she heard that night. By the end of the meeting she was filled with compassion for the Chicago anarchists and convinced that they were innocent. She realized that if they were put to death, it would be for their political ideals—not in the Russia she had fled, but right here in the country that supposedly guaranteed free speech and free opinion to everyone.

Several weeks later Emma came across the anarchist newspaper *Freiheit,* which means "freedom," in the home of a friend. It was written in German and published in New York by the famous anarchist John Most. The paper was filled with scathing denunciations of the Chicago trial. Emma read every word, spellbound. After that, she read every copy of *Freiheit* she could lay her hands on. She sent for all the pamphlets advertised in the paper that had anything to do with the Haymarket Trial and pored over them.

The case was appealed to the Supreme Court, but all appeals were rejected. At the last minute the governor of Illinois commuted to life imprisonment two of the death sentences. One other of the condemned men committed suicide in his cell. Four were left.

On November 11, 1887, more than a year after the trial and nine months after Emma's unfortunate marriage, the four who were left were taken to the gallows and hanged. As the nooses were lowered around their necks, two of them were heard to cry, "Hurray for anarchy!"

That tragic November day became known as Black Friday. On that day Emma was with her sister Helena. Helena spent the day quietly weeping, but Emma was too numb even to cry. That evening in their father's house a few people gathered to discuss the awful news. Emma sat alone. Suddenly the voice of one of the women, arrogant and shrill, intruded into Emma's mourning.

"What's all this lament about? The men were murderers. It is well they were hanged!"

Without an instant's hesitation, Emma leaped for the woman's throat. Someone pulled her away from the woman, but there was no stopping her. Wriggling free, she grabbed a pitcher of water from the table and flung it with all her might in the woman's face. "Out, out, or I will kill you!" she screamed. Then she fell to the floor, hysterical.

When hours later she regained control of herself, she felt that she was a new, a different person. The hanging of the anarchists caused in her a change so profound that it was like a religious conversion. For the rest of her life, she would remember that Black Friday as the day of her social awakening, and the martyred men as "the most decisive influence of my existence."

Actually, though, Emma already believed in many of the ideals of the martyrs long before the Haymarket Affair. Her whole life had been preparing her for this conversion. From her earliest childhood she had been painfully sensitive to the injustice everywhere around her. She had suffered with the brutalized peasants, with the persecuted Jews, with the tyrannized students, with the martyred Russian revolutionaries, and with the exploited workers. She longed for a different kind of society—the kind envisioned by the populists, the socialists, and now she learned, by the anarchists. She had hoped to find it in America, but she had been bitterly disappointed.

Until she became engrossed in the Haymarket Affair, her models of active revolutionaries had come from books. The people she knew personally who shared her dream of a radically different society were students or teachers or workers, whose daily lives were much like the lives of any students or teachers or workers. Their radicalism was mainly in their talk. Now Emma had before her eyes *real* revolutionaries, people whose ideas and dreams directed every action of their lives, even to their deaths. She began to revere the Haymarket martyrs as she had revered the assassins of the czar.

As she followed the Haymarket case and pored through the *Freiheit,* Emma saw that not only was there a radical way to think, but there was a radical movement to join, and a radical life to live. She was converted not so much by a set of ideas as by a vision of life.

After the Chicago anarchists were hanged, she found that she could no longer be content only to sympathize and think with the revolutionaries. She would have to *act* as a revolutionary; she would have to become a revolutionary.

Remembering the day of her conversion years later, she wrote:

> I had a distinct sensation that something new and wonderful had been born in my soul. A great ideal, a burning faith, a determination to dedicate myself to the memory of my martyred comrades, to make their cause my own, to make known to the world their beautiful lives and heroic deaths. . . . My mind was made up. I would go to New York . . . [and] prepare myself for my new task.

Emma was not the sort of person who had ever done anything halfway. She could not be a halfway radical either. She had never been able to accept abuse or injustice without putting up a fight. Now she would carry her fight into society. With the enormous energy and enthusiasm that characterized almost everything she did, Emma prepared to dedicate her life to fighting, like the Haymarket martyrs, for anarchism.

5

What is Anarchism?

I heartily accept the motto—"That government is best which governs least" . . . carried out, it finally amounts to this, which also I believe— "That government is best which governs not at all."

—HENRY DAVID THOREAU

The Haymarket martyrs were not the only ones to be put to death shouting "Hurray for anarchy!" In France, in Italy, in Russia, in Spain, men and women had died on the gallows or would die before the firing squad with "anarchy" their final word.

What was the anarchist ideal for which these men and women had been put to death? Why did some people want to destroy it, while others were willing to die for it?

Probably everyone agrees that society could be set up more fairly than it is. Everywhere in the world, some people are rich while others are poor; some people have a lot of power while others have none. Knowing this, from time to time people have tried to imagine other social systems that would be much fairer than the systems we have. Some of them have only imagined other systems; some have tried to put their systems into practice. But all of them have been *social idealists* because they have all had in mind some ideal system, better than any that now exists.

Anarchism is one of these ideal social systems. Springing from the same impulse to set up a fair society, it is like populism, socialism, and democracy in some ways. In other ways it is different from each of them.

Very simply, anarchism is a political and social system opposed to all forms of government based on force. An anarchist society would have no laws, no lawmakers, no officials, no police, no armies, no institutions, or even any customs or traditions that people would be forced to obey against their will.

Then how would an anarchist society work without government? In an anarchist society every single person would be at liberty to do as he or she pleased. Being free, anarchists believe, people would choose to cooperate with each other voluntarily for the good of everyone. A word often used to describe this main feature of anarchism is *libertarian*. An anarchist society is based on individual *liberty,* not government *authority* or *force.*

Some people believe that without laws, and a government to enforce the laws, life would be nothing but disorder and chaos. They believe that if people were completely free to do whatever they liked, the strong and the vicious would prey on the weak and the innocent. They believe that everyone would compete with everyone else, and that people would think only of their own advantage, regardless of how their actions affected others. They believe that people would give in to their destructive impulses unless some enforceable law prevented it. As the English philosopher Thomas Hobbes put it: without government, people would live in a permanent state of "war of everyone against everyone." This is one widely held view of human nature and society. For those who hold this view, "anarchy" and "anarchism" are synonymous with political chaos, or, at best, political confusion.

Most anarchists hold a different view of human nature. They believe that people are basically good and cooperative. They believe that if people were left completely free to do as they please, they would choose to control whatever selfish and destructive impulses they might have. They believe that people would work together to produce what they need to live because it is obviously more sensible and more useful to work *with* each other than *against* each other. Anarchists point out that it has always been because most people willingly help each other most of the time that the work of the world manages to get done in the end. People can and do solve their own problems and get their work done for themselves very nicely without being told what to do by some outsider or forced to do it by some law.

In fact, warn the anarchists, laws and governments achieve the very opposite of what they pretend. Claiming to establish "law and order," governments put some people in a position of power over other people. This inequality is hopelessly unjust. And it is because of this basic and widespread injustice that crime and disorder spring up in society. Then a vicious circle begins: to combat the disorder, governments use more force, imposing more laws and restrictions, which create even more injustice, and ultimately more disorder—leading to still more force, more laws, more injustice, more disorder.

Anarchists are not against order, as many people believe. They are only against imposing order *by force* or *threat of force.* They oppose the force used by governments against their own citizens through police, and against the citizens of other nations through armies. They believe that order would certainly prevail in a world where people were free to do as they pleased, because people would choose to make and follow certain rules for their own mutual benefit. That is a very different matter from being forced to follow rules imposed from outside for someone else's benefit.

The governments of most modern national States, with their vast bureaucracies, for instance, impose innumerable rules on every aspect of life. Except for the rich, most people are not free to decide even such basic things as what they shall learn in school, which partly determines what sorts of jobs they shall have. The populace is regulated "to within an inch of its life," writes a modern American anarchist.

Anarchists' extreme distrust of government seems to many people a reasonable attitude toward governments run by a few people at the top, but an unreasonable attitude toward democratic governments. For don't democracies, in which the citizens elect their representatives, make only those rules the people want?

Anarchists say, emphatically, no! Even under the best of governments, people must, under threat of force, obey laws made by strangers. These strangers, these "representatives," live very different sorts of lives from those of the people who elect them. They know little about the problems or needs of their constituents. The laws governing everyone are made by a mere handful of people, the elected officials, who want above all to keep themselves in power. *Any* government, democratic or not, say the anarchists, must be unjust because some people rule over others. And anarchists, with rare exceptions, refuse to have anything to do with politics, elections, public office, political parties, or any aspect of government.

The first man to call himself an anarchist was a Frenchman named Pierre-Joseph Proudhon (1809–1865). Proudhon railed angrily against the senseless intrusion of government into peoples' daily lives. "To be governed," he wrote,

> is to be watched over, inspected, spied on, directed, legislated at, regulated, docketed, indoctrinated, preached at, controlled, assessed, weighed, censored, ordered about, by men who have neither the right nor the knowledge nor the virtue. To be governed means . . . to be, on the pretext of the general interest, taxed, drilled, held to ransom, exploited, monopolized, extorted, squeezed, hoaxed, robbed; then at the least

resistance, at the first word of complaint, to be re-
pressed, fined, abused, annoyed, followed, bullied,
beaten, disarmed, garrotted, imprisoned, machine-
gunned, judged, condemned, deported, flayed, sold, betrayed, and finally mocked, ridiculed, insulted, dishon-
ored. That's government, that's its justice, that's its
morality!

Anarchists are not the only people who have been
suspicious of governmental power. The founders of the
United States were themselves so distrustful of governmental power that they tried to limit it in the Constitution. They wrote the Constitution so that the lawmakers and law enforcers, the state governments and the
federal government, could check and limit each other's
power. The Bill of Rights was added to the Constitution to protect individuals and minorities from the tremendous power of the majority. But these limitations
written into the Constitution did not go nearly far
enough for some Americans. Carrying their native distrust of government to its final conclusion, certain
Americans became anarchists, some before ever reading
the works of Proudhon and the other European anarchists.

While these native American anarchists were chiefly
interested in opposing the power of government, European anarchists were equally interested in opposing the
power of the rich. For it is not only through their governments and laws that the people in power—the
establishment—control others. They exert control
through their economic power as well.

In most modern societies, including our own, for all the talk about equality, some people are rich and respected while others are poor and despised. Some countries have a high standard of living, while in other countries most people live in poverty. It is all terribly unfair, yet it continues. Why? Surely the world is rich enough that no one anywhere should be hungry. Yet year after year, millions of people actually starve, some even in the United States, the richest country of all. Why?

Some anarchists, particularly certain of the American groups, have blamed all such injustice on government alone. But according to most anarchists, such terrible inequality continues because of our present economic system. Our system, known as capitalism, practically guarantees inequality. For under the capitalist economic system most of society's riches—the resources crucial for producing the necessities of life—are owned and run for the private profit of relatively few people or companies. Everyone else, including those who do most of the work, is more or less used by the few at the top.

Defenders of capitalism admit that under capitalism the resources are run by the few—but for the benefit of everyone. Capitalism, they say, is the most efficient system. Under it many workers live very comfortably indeed. Anarchists find freedom and equality more important than material comfort, and happiness more important than efficiency. In any case, though many workers may be well off under capitalism, many others barely manage to survive.

The Russian-born Michael Bakunin (1814–1876) was

the man who, more than any other, built anarchism into a large, powerful movement in Europe. He wrote: "From the moment that property rights became generally accepted, society had to split into two parts: on the 'one hand the property-owning, privileged minority, exploiting organized and forced labor, and on the other hand millions of proletarians [workers]."

Bakunin saw the national State as the chief enemy of liberty, but he recognized that the power of the State rested on its economic power. "Political power and wealth are inseparable," he wrote. "Those who have the power have the means to gain wealth, and . . . those who are wealthy must become strong."

Anarchists are not the first people to see the unfairness of capitalism. Among social idealists there have always been many who imagined a society in which people owned things jointly, "communally," instead of privately. This broad "communist" idea is behind many of the aims of populism, socialism, and anarchism alike. During the nineteenth century, factories all over Europe were being run on the labor of masses of wretchedly paid workers. In response, certain social idealists developed penetrating criticisms of modern capitalist society. Instead of capitalism, these critics proposed a system in which society's riches would be owned communally—by the community—rather than by certain individuals or corporations.

The most brilliant of these critics was Karl Marx, the German-born leader of the European socialist movement. Both anarchists and socialists adopted Marx's ideas. Both held that society's riches—the land, factories, natural resources, institutions—must be turned over to the people who work them before there can be any real economic equality. For many years anarchists and socialists all worked together against capitalism in one growing, united, international movement. They overlooked their disagreements. Yet there was a basic disagreement between them that eventually split the entire social-revolutionary movement apart.

For while most anarchists and socialists agree that the capitalist society should be replaced by some sort of communal society, they disagree about what sort. The socialists would put all society's resources under the control of a strong central government. It would be a government run by and for the workers, but a government all the same. Anarchists want to have no central control of anything at all. In their ideal society the people who use the resources can decide by themselves how to manage them. Any government, even a socialist one, the anarchists say, needlessly restricts individual liberty. Bakunin and Marx and their followers hotly disputed these matters until, by the 1870's, the anarchists and socialists could no longer work together.

Unlike the socialists, the anarchists believe that control of society must be totally decentralized. Each community of people with the same interests should be able to make its own rules for itself, without any outside interference. It makes no difference whether a community is one of workers in a factory, farmers tilling an area of land, teachers and students in a school, people living together in a neighborhood, consumers in a store, or actors in a theater. They must all be free to run their own communities for themselves. Certainly the members of a group will know how to run their affairs better than outsiders. Knowing what they want, they will not need outside lawmakers or administrators or police.

People with the same aims doing the same things form natural communities. To work together, they form working communities, or as anarchists call them, *collectives.* These are nothing like the arbitrary communities imposed by governments, called nations or States. Humanity is international.

Some collectives will be tiny, some will be huge, but all must be run "collectively" by the members themselves.

The constructive aspects of anarchism were emphasized by Peter Kropotkin (1842–1921), a Russian who, after Bakunin died, became the leading spokesman of this philosophy. In his writings he described how small communities of free individuals could work harmoniously together to produce enough of everything for everyone. His books, with such titles as *Mutual Aid* and *The Conquest of Bread,* were humane and reasonable. Ultimately it was his view of anarchism that Emma adopted.

To rid society of government, of capitalism, of force, of social privilege, of economic inequality—these are the things anarchists dream of doing. Until they are done, anarchists believe, the libertarian communal society can never be. How will they be done? Anarchists, like all social-revolutionary groups, have a single answer: through revolution. A revolution—a completely clean sweep, a total change in every single institution in society—that is the only way they see to bring the ideal social system into the real world.

Most anarchists feel that the revolution cannot be imposed on the mass of people, but that it must be desired by them. Yet different anarchists have emphasized different ways of making the revolution desirable and possible. Some have thought it must be violent and bloody, since those in power do not give up their power readily. Some have believed it could be accomplished peacefully, through persuasion. Some have held it would require efforts of both kinds.

Those who believe it must be violent point out that people of every political opinion believe in using violence under some circumstances. All governments, for example, stay in power through their armies and police. Certain anarchists have felt that occasional violent dramatic acts could be useful to publicize society's injustices. These acts, called "propaganda by deed," might be anything from the destruction of records, such as draft records, to the assassination of the head of a government, such as the czar. "Propaganda by deed" has always been intended to supplement "propaganda by word," especially in countries where censorship has made spoken or written propaganda difficult.

Those anarchists who believe it possible to bring about the revolution peaceably still want action. They do not rely on the vote; voting out one group and voting in another is, for them, only an exchange of one government for another and therefore of one evil for another. They rely instead on "direct action" by the working class to popularize the revolution. Strikes, boycotts, mass demonstrations—these are the favorite tactics of anarchists. Consequently, the anarchist movement has often been closely tied to the labor movement, as it was in Chicago at the time of the Haymarket Affair.

Most anarchists are ready to accept some violence during the moment of the revolution when power changes hands. Still, not all, or even most, anarchists favor violent methods of propaganda. Since a number of notorious assassinations have been committed by anarchists, in the minds of many people violence and anarchism go hand in hand.

Bakunin himself took part in several violent rebellions for which he spent many terrible years in prison. Although he believed that when it came the great revolution would be a "spontaneous" uprising of the people, he was always ready to speed it up by joining any local uprising he knew about. His eagerness to risk his life for the revolution time after time made him a heroic figure to his followers.

Peter Kropotkin was a very different sort of man. Unlike the fiery Bakunin, Kropotkin was a gentle, peace-loving scholar. Born a Russian prince, he had early renounced his title and given away his property. Considered a "saint" by his admirers, he spread the doctrines of anarchism not by joining rebellions but by writing books and articles and organizing anarchist conferences. But even the gentle Kropotkin believed that "to expect a *social* revolution to come like a Christmas box, without being heralded by small acts of revolt and insurrections, is to cherish a vain hope." Since the State always uses force to maintain its power, force would probably be necessary to overthrow it, conceded Kropotkin. After that, no force would ever be used.

After 1880, during the time Emma turned anarchist, many violent deeds were committed in the name of anarchism. In 1892 alone there were more than one thousand dynamitings in Europe and almost five hundred in America. Several heads of State were assassinated; others were afraid for their lives. By terrifying people these deeds often made more enemies for anarchism than converts. They contributed to the popular but false impression that all anarchists believe in terror.

During the early days of the labor-union movement in America, there was a lot of violent fighting between labor and management. Most of it was started by management—who put down strikes by force—and not by workers. But once the association of anarchism with violence took hold of the popular imagination, it stuck. After that anarchists were apt to be blamed by the public for all political acts of violence, even for those in which they had no part. And anarchists were frequently persecuted, as they were in America after the Haymarket bombing.

Emma Goldman had been something of a rebel all her life. As she learned of the doctrines of anarchism, she was irresistibly drawn to them. She had already begun sympathizing with revolution in her student days in St. Petersburg. She already knew from experience the atrocities a strong government can commit against large groups of people—against the peasants and Jews of Russia, against the immigrants and radicals of America. She already knew, through every job she had ever had, how the poor suffer under capitalism. The ideas of anarchism seemed confirmed by everything that had ever been done to her.

When the Chicago anarchists were hanged, Emma's love for them as martyrs and her fascination with their theories mixed and mingled and finally became one. Embracing their ideals as her own, she became an anarchist for life.

The time had come to act. Though she had been unhappy in her brief marriage before the Haymarket hangings, she had not been able to end it. Divorce was a disgrace. Now she decided to leave Jacob Kershner, disgrace or no. Her family threw her out; scandalized people avoided her in the street. But she got her divorce anyway, with only Helena to back her up.

She moved to New Haven, Connecticut, where a job in a corset factory had been offered her. Within a year, however, she was back in Rochester, ill from overwork and loneliness. Feeling utterly defeated, she even returned briefly to Jacob.

Of course, nothing in Rochester had changed. Seeing how futile it was to try to live, as she called it, "a patched life," once again she prepared to leave. She took a quick course in dressmaking, scraped together the money to buy a sewing machine, borrowed cash from Helena for a one-way train ticket to New York, and packed her bag again.

The second time she left, she left for good. On August 15, 1889, newly turned twenty, Emma kissed Helena goodbye, boarded a train for New York, and launched her new life as an ardent full-time anarchist.

6

A Radical Life

All the world is on the tip of the tongue.
—YIDDISH PROVERB

It was a hot Sunday morning in August 1889 when Emma arrived, at long last, in New York City. She checked her sewing machine—her means to independence—in the Forty-second Street station's baggage room. Then she started walking downtown, past the glamorous hub of the great city toward the densely crowded Lower East Side immigrant slum.

In her small bag Emma had $5.00 and three addresses, her only resources for New York. One address was of a married aunt; one was of a young anarchist named Solotaroff whom she had once heard speak in

New Haven; and one was the address of John Most's anarchist newspaper *Freiheit,* which she had read so avidly in Rochester. She had no friends, but she wasn't worried. She knew she would make her way.

First Emma went looking for her aunt. The busy ghetto streets, lined with pushcart peddlers hawking their wares in Yiddish and Russian, were as crowded as the ghetto of St. Petersburg, and the people seemed as poor. Picking her way among the ragged children playing in the streets and on the crowded sidewalks, Emma found the tenement building where her aunt lived. Though her aunt offered to put her up for a few nights in her cramped quarters, Emma saw at once that she didn't really want her to stay. Pretending a friend was expecting her, Emma left in search of Solotaroff, whose name was second on her list. When she finally found him a few blocks away, he treated her like an old welcome friend, even though they had met only once. Political ties, evidently, could be stronger than family ones.

Solotaroff took her around to Sachs's Café on Suffolk Street—the local hangout for radicals, poets, and scholars—in the heart of the Lower East Side. Inside there seemed to be as much going on as there was outside on the crowded street. The café was packed with lively, spirited people all gesticulating and arguing in many languages—Russian, German, Yiddish, English. All the famous radicals were there, talking intensely between swallows of beer. As Solotaroff pointed them out to Emma, one after another, Emma eagerly took it all in. If there was any single place in New York City to begin her plunge into the radical life, surely, she thought, it was here.

After they were settled at a table, Solotaroff introduced Emma to two radical sisters, Helen and Anna Minkin, who he knew were looking for a roommate. Emma, said the sisters, would do perfectly. Now her biggest problem, where to live, was out of the way.

All of a sudden Emma heard someone call for an "extra large steak! Extra cup of coffee!"

"Who is that glutton?" Emma asked.

"That is Alexander Berkman," Solotaroff laughed. "He rarely has enough money for much food. When he has, he eats Sachs out of his supplies. I'll introduce you to him."

Alexander Berkman, nicknamed Sasha, was a revolutionary Russian immigrant, barely eighteen. He had been expelled from school in Russia because of an essay he wrote explaining why he did not believe in God. He had the neck and chest of a giant, a high, studious forehead, and serious, intelligent eyes. Meeting him, Emma sensed that something wonderful and important was about to happen to her.

"John Most is speaking tonight. Do you want to come to hear him?" Sasha asked Emma after the introductions. John Most, the editor of *Freiheit,* was the third name on Emma's list! It was too much of a coincidence to let pass. Of course she would go to hear him.

On their way to the hall where Most was to speak, Emma stumbled. Sasha gripped her tightly to keep her from falling. "I have saved your life," he said, smiling.

"I hope I may be able to save yours someday," she replied.

John Most was even more remarkable as a speaker than as a writer. He was unquestionably one of the most celebrated radicals in America. At one time he had almost single-handedly rallied the social-revolutionaries in America into an organized movement through his newspaper, his speeches, and his tireless organizing efforts. He had come to America six years before, straight from an English prison. There he had served sixteen months at hard labor for an article he had written praising the assassination of Czar Alexander II of Russia. It had been his fifth prison sentence. A follower of Bakunin, he was a strong advocate of propaganda by deed. Through his newspaper he encouraged such acts, even printing instructions for the manufacture of dynamite bombs. His hatred of the evils of capitalism glowed hotter in him than a love of mankind. But with his forceful personality and his bitter eloquence, he served the cause of radicalism as well as many a gentler man.

A slender man with a great full beard, Most had a face hideously disfigured by some childhood disease. Seeing him, Emma was overcome with revulsion. After he began to speak, however, her revulsion turned to something like awe. His furious invective transformed him. That night Most discussed the Haymarket Affair, angrily denouncing the social conditions that had caused it. Emma was quite overwhelmed by his eloquence. He seemed to have a magical tongue, made all the more potent by his scathing message. He was, she said, "a man apart; the most remarkable in all the world." When Sasha took her to meet Most after the lecture, she was too nervous to speak to him. And when she returned to her new home with the Minkin sisters that night, she couldn't close her eyes, so much had happened to her in that single day.

The next morning, as on many mornings after, Sasha was waiting to see her. Out of a job himself, he offered to take her around the city. Together they set off to recover her sewing machine from the checkroom on Forty-second Street.

In the following days Emma and Sasha spent many hours together. They told each other about themselves —of their young lives in Russia, of the experiences that had moved them, the books that had influenced them, what they wanted to make of their lives. Emma thought she had never met a man more dedicated, more principled, than Sasha. Nothing in the world was more important to him than the Cause, the revolution. For the Cause he seemed willing to make any sacrifice. "A good anarchist is one who lives only for the Cause and gives everything to it," he said with solemn conviction. Surely he was one of those rare souls who might be chosen to do great deeds.

Emma did not believe herself capable of such single-mindedness. Though she, too, was determined to devote herself to the cause of anarchism, she cared about other things besides. Love, friendship, a beautiful sunset, wild flowers, music—it seemed that her life would be unbearable without "beautiful radiant things." Everyone, she thought, is entitled to a little joy.

But Sasha disagreed. He said it was wrong for an anarchist "to enjoy luxuries when the people live in poverty"; wrong to be moved by personal sentiment. Perhaps, he suggested, Emma was too romantic and sentimental to be a revolutionary.

Emma argued for her view, but she felt at the same time that Sasha was right. His uncompromising fervor, his purity, his complete selflessness, filled her with admiration. She would try to learn from him his revolutionary ethic. Not yet able to trust completely her own feelings, she vowed to try to purify herself and understand *his* revolutionary right and wrong.

She told him of her own resolve after the Haymarket hangings.

"We are comrades," he said, gripping Emma's arm until it hurt. "Let us be friends too—let us work together."

It was not long before Emma went around to the *Freiheit* office. John Most gave her work addressing envelopes. Despite his gruff, almost angry, manner, he seemed pleased that Emma had come to see him. He suggested that after work they go out to dinner together.

At dinner the fiery old anarchist, the man whom the Rochester newspapers had characterized as the devil himself, seemed transformed into an entirely different person. His bitterness and fire seemed to dissolve in the wine he drank, and in their place Emma found a warm and sympathetic friend. Emma told him how she had come to New York to devote her life to anarchism and that she had sought him out, as the "leading spirit of anarchism," to ask his guidance and advice.

Most grew thoughtful. Finally, he told Emma to think carefully about her decision. "The path of anarchism is steep and painful," he said; "the price is exacting. Few men are ready to pay it, most women not at all."

"No women?" Emma asked. "Are there no outstanding anarchist women in America?"

"None at all, only stupids," he replied. "Most of the girls come to the meetings to snatch up a man; then both vanish."

Emma was shocked. Why was Most, who as a revolutionary ought to have known better, saying such insulting things about women? She thought he must be teasing.

He went on. Emma, he said, could be the exception. If she were really certain of her decision, if she were really in earnest, he promised to guide her. He would tell her what books to read; he would give her work to do. He would educate her and mold her future.

Willingly, Emma became his protégée. That night, as she climbed the stairs to the Minkin apartment, she felt that "the charm of Most was upon me."

A short time later John Most left New York on a lecture tour. While he was gone Emma got a job in another corset factory. She lasted only a few weeks there, however, before the strain became unbearable. Through a bit of luck she learned from a friend about a job she could do at home, sewing blouses on her own sewing machine. It would be easier to work at home than in a factory, though she would have to leave the Minkins and find a room of her own. She found one near Sachs's Café for $3.00 a month, and set up her machine. Soon she was making as much money as she had made in the corset factory, and her time was her own.

One evening after John Most returned Emma told him a story of her childhood. She told it so movingly that Most declared she had a great and natural talent for speaking. He said she was capable of moving audiences and that she must begin to speak in public, to lecture for the movement. He said he would make a great speaker of her—"to take my place when I am gone."

Emma followed his advice exactly, beginning by practicing her speaking on small groups of immigrant workers. Though at first she was frightened and self-conscious, to her listeners she sounded calm and convincing. She read the books Most suggested and worshipfully repeated his words. He was pleased with her progress, and she was thrilled to be able to please him.

Most was her idol, but it was Sasha whom she grew to love as the months went by. On November 11, the anniversary of that Black Friday when the Haymarket martyrs were hanged, she and Sasha went to a rally in their honor. Sasha had been as deeply affected by the Chicago hangings as Emma had been. He had vowed when they died to avenge them. After the rally Emma and he walked silently back to Emma's room. Each felt the other's reverence for the martyrs whose deaths they were commemorating that night. They were united in reverence. They felt a mysterious closeness to each other.

Once, when Emma had told Sasha about her wretched marriage and divorce, she had said she believed marriage to be wrong. She believed it was wrong to tie people together for life, wrong to try to force love. "If I ever love a man again," she had told him, "I will give myself to him without being bound by the rabbi or the law. And when that love dies, I will leave without permission."

Sasha had admired her purity of feeling and her resolution. All true revolutionaries, he had told her, had discarded marriage for freedom. Freedom strengthened love, he said.

That night they became lovers. Emma knew that thereafter their lives were linked together for all time. Their love would be stronger than any marriage.

They took an apartment together on Forty-second Street. Its four small rooms were large enough to accommodate two of their closest friends. Helen Minkin and Fedya, an artist friend of Sasha's whom Emma liked very much, moved in with them.

From the start they ran their household like a true commune, sharing everything. Each member gave all that he had and took only what he needed. Only rarely did Fedya sell a painting, but the others kept him steadily supplied with paints and canvases all the same. Emma kept house and sewed blouses on her machine, while Helen and Sasha worked at factory jobs. Together they attended meetings and worked for the movement.

Soon Most decided it was time for Emma's first lecture tour. The other members of the commune insisted Emma stop sewing and devote every minute of her time to preparing her lectures. They even took over all the housekeeping chores. The Cause came first, they said.

On her tour Emma was to lecture in German to immigrants in Rochester, Buffalo, and Cleveland. Most had selected her topic for her and had given her his own notes to memorize. With his ideas and her own sense of the dramatic, he said, she was bound to be a success.

Just before she was to leave, Emma was shaken by a disturbing idea. She suddenly realized that it would be useless and foolish to memorize Most's notes. To be a good speaker, she would have to speak for herself, and not simply parrot the ideas of her teacher. She would have to be independent in her anarchism as in everything else. Wasn't that, after all, the core of anarchism?

She boarded the train for Rochester filled with uncertainty. Only six months had passed since she had left Rochester, but she felt herself years older. She hoped her return would be triumphant.

When she faced her first public audience the following day, her mind went blank. She could not remember her notes or even the subject Most had picked for her. And then, as she recalled it, "something strange happened. . . . Words I had never heard myself utter before came pouring forth, faster and faster. They came with passionate intensity. . . . The audience had vanished, the hall itself had disappeared; I was conscious only of my own words, of my ecstatic song." She spoke of the brutal past and of the radiant anarchist society to come. She spoke in her own words of her own vision. When she stopped she was overwhelmed with applause.

She knew she had been right to discard Most's ideas

for her own. Now she knew, as Most had known, that she, Emma Goldman, had the power to sway people with the magic of her words. Her own words. She wept for joy.

As soon as she returned to New York she told Most of her new attitude. She explained that for her own sake and for the movement's sake she could no longer follow him blindly.

He turned on her, enraged at her "betrayal." He said he would rather cut her straight out of his heart forever than have her as a lukewarm friend. "Who is not with me is against me!" he shouted.

Surely those were not the words of an anarchist, thought Emma. Now she was even more doubtful of Most's right to guide her. Not only did he fail to respect her own ideas, but he ridiculed her right to have them and he even began to insult her as a "mere female." It was intolerable.

Eventually, in the years that followed, Emma came to feel that an anarchist group which Most considered his rival and enemy was closer than Most's to her own idea of anarchism. The group was called Autonomie, and it was inspired by the works of the gentle Peter Kropotkin. For them as for Emma, absolute liberty for the individual and the independence of every group were the moving ideas of anarchism. John Most, powered by fury, stressed instead the fight against the evils of the present system. He followed Bakunin more than Kropotkin. Brilliant and rugged warrior that he was, he did not always allow freedom and independence even to his own followers. Though Emma had gone to school at

Most's feet, receiving her training as a revolutionary from him, she felt her schooldays were over. Despite Most's anger, she and Sasha joined Autonomie. However, she continued to work closely with Most, right up until 1891, when he served another prison term for a provocative speech. But she had moved beyond his teachings. She was no longer an apprentice. She was ready to stand on her own. If she took her inspiration from anyone, it was from Sasha, whose purity and dedication were unmatched.

After the success of her initial speaking tour, Emma plunged into the work of the movement. She was the major organizer of women in the great cloakmaker strike of 1889. She led the anarchists at the New York May Day demonstration in 1891—a demonstration supporting the labor movement all over the world. She arranged countless meetings and lectures on anarchism; she agitated among the unions; she distributed reams of leaflets.

The little commune moved and regrouped, according to the needs of the moment. For a while Emma, Sasha, Fedya, and the Minkin sisters moved the commune to New Haven, Connecticut, where Sasha had been offered a chance to learn the printing trade. There the group continued its anarchist work. Though the women had to take factory jobs, everyone was still able to do enough organizing and lecturing to make the commune the center for a growing anarchist movement in New Haven. Only the sudden serious illness of Anna Minkin sent them all scurrying back to New York.

Living together as they did, Emma and Fedya began

after a while to love each other too. Emma's feeling for Sasha was as strong as ever, but with Fedya she shared a joy in the beauties of nature and art for which there was no room in Sasha's zealous life. She still loved roses too. When she and Fedya told Sasha how they felt, he accepted the news easily. He told them that he believed in their freedom to love. Jealousy, he said, was a base, possessive feeling which deserved no place in an anarchist's heart. People are not property to own and possess. With Sasha's blessing, Emma and Fedya too became lovers. After that, the three comrades lived together with more consideration and understanding of each other than ever before.

Together the three made a pact. They swore to dedicate themselves "to the Cause in some supreme deed; to die together if necessary, or to continue to live and work for the ideal for which one of us might have to give his life."

Together they would serve the Cause any way they could until the moment came for their "supreme deed."

7

Homestead: The Supreme Deed

I do not think I shall die, but whether I do or not, the Company will pursue the same policy, and it will win.
—HENRY CLAY FRICK, AFTER BEING WOUNDED BY
AN ASSASSIN'S BULLET

Reports of a new wave of terrorism in Russia convinced the three revolutionary comrades that they must return to their native land. There, they believed, they could best serve the cause of international anarchism. But traveling to Russia would require a large sum of money, and they had none. It was to make money fast for their new project that Emma, Sasha, and Fedya found themselves in spring 1892 serving coffee, cake, and ice-cream sodas to the people of Worcester, Massachusetts. Temporarily they had turned capitalist.

Fedya had led them to Massachusetts in the first place

in pursuit of a job, but the job had not worked out. Instead, with money borrowed from their landlord, they had invested in ingredients and equipment and opened an ice-cream parlor. Although it was still too early in the season for big ice-cream sales, with good luck, good coffee, and hard work, the three comrades had already begun to make a profit.

They had just paid back their debt to their landlord and were beginning to save a little money for themselves, when something happened in Pennsylvania to make them change their plans.

The steelworkers of Homestead, Pennsylvania, had been negotiating a new labor contract with their employer, the Carnegie Steel Company. The workers' union, at the time the strongest union in the country, was the Amalgamated Iron and Steel Workers of America. The company was represented by its chairman, Henry Clay Frick.

Frick was a shrewd businessman, already on his way to becoming one of America's leading millionaires. He was unscrupulous in his climb to power. When, for example, he saw an unflattering cartoon about himself in a Pittsburgh newspaper, he said to his secretary, "This won't do at all. Find out who owns this paper and buy it."

During the negotiations with the steelworkers Frick suddenly announced without warning that the talks were over. From then on, he said, the Homestead steel plant would operate as a nonunion plant. He would hire the workers as individuals, but not as members of a union.

Now the dispute was no longer over wages; it was over the workers' right to organize into a union. When the union workers refused to work without a union contract, Frick fired them all, locked them out of the plant, and made plans to hire nonunion workers in their place. "I will never recognize the union, never, never!" Frick said. The workers turned the lockout into a strike and prepared to prevent strikebreakers from entering the plant. The battle between workers and owners was on.

Meanwhile, in Worcester, Emma, Sasha, and Fedya followed the news from Homestead closely. As the situation grew tense, they began to feel they were needed in Homestead more urgently than in Russia. Russia, Sasha said, had many revolutionaries. But who was there in America besides themselves? When they read that the families of the strikers were being evicted from their company-owned houses, and that Frick had hired an army of private Pinkerton detectives to "protect his property," the trio resolved to go to Homestead themselves. They would compose a manifesto to urge the strikers on. They would try to make the workers see that they must strike not only for their own union and for the moment, but "for all time, for a free life, for anarchism."

Once they decided, they acted quickly. At closing time that very night, the three anarchists turned over the keys of their ice-cream parlor and all its contents to their landlord. The landlord thought them mad to abandon such a promising business, but their minds were made up. With only the $75.00 they had taken in from that day's customers, they left hastily for New York on an early-morning train. The next day, in blazing Russian prose, they composed their manifesto. As soon as they could get it translated into English and printed, they would take it to Homestead.

Once again, events intervened to change their plans. On July 6, in the middle of the night, three hundred armed Pinkerton strikebreakers on two dark barges came silently down the Monongahela River from Pittsburgh and tried to dock behind the Homestead plant. The strikers were waiting for them. Incensed that armed hirelings should be employed against them, they prevented the barges from landing and tried to set them on fire. A terrible, bloody battle broke out, in which three Pinkertons and ten strikers were killed, and hundreds more were injured.

The entire nation was stunned by the events at Homestead. Not only organized labor, but Congress and private citizens everywhere were shaken by the spectacle of a private army being employed to settle a labor dispute. Even some of the antilabor press criticized Frick's actions. In the following months the whole question of the rights of labor and the rights of management, human rights and property rights, would for the first time be officially discussed in the United States.

When Emma, Sasha, and Fedya read about the Homestead battle, they felt that passing out a manifesto was far too feeble a gesture for them to make. The time for propaganda by words was past. The time had come for propaganda by deed. The whole country was aroused against Frick's resort to violence; the whole nation was watching Homestead. It was the perfect psychological moment, they felt, for a great and terrible act of propaganda.

As soon as Sasha proposed it, they all agreed. They must assassinate Frick—as their Russian heroes had assassinated the czar. In one momentous act, one supreme deed, they would avenge the murder of the Homestead strikers and rally the nation behind the workers.

Sasha insisted that he go to Homestead alone, though Emma and Fedya begged to be allowed to join him. It was for him to commit the act, Sasha said, and for Emma to explain it to the world. She was the orator among them. Emma longed to risk her life for the Cause with Sasha and share in his fate, but she recognized the sense in his plan.

Sasha decided on a time-bomb for a weapon. For a week, while Emma stood guard, Sasha experimented with dynamite in the apartment of a friend. What if there were an accident and the apartment blew up? The end, they rashly believed, justified any means. The end they were serving was the Cause of the people. Later they would feel differently, but at the time Emma still believed that a few innocent lives might well have to be sacrificed.

Though Sasha carefully followed John Most's published instructions for bomb making, when the day came for him to test his bomb, it failed to explode. Too much money and time had been lost to allow him to begin again. There was only one thing left to do, Sasha said. He must shoot Frick.

Again, he insisted on going to Pennsylvania alone.

He knew he would probably pay for his deed with his life. Why sacrifice three anarchist lives when one would do? The three conspirators had only $15.00 left among them—just enough to get one person to Pennsylvania, with a dollar left over for one day's rent and food. Sasha would still need another $20.00 for a gun and for a suit of clothes in which to enter Frick's office without arousing suspicion. He left it up to Emma and Fedya to get the money. They were to get it any way they could.

With an iron will and a tender heart, that evening Sasha boarded the train for Pittsburgh. Emma stood on the bottom step of the train, her hand in his. The lovers believed they were seeing each other for the last time.

"My Sailor Girl," Sasha whispered, bending down to her. It was his old pet-name for Emma. "You will be with me to the last."

He let go of her hand, and the train steamed out of the station.

That night, lying in bed, Emma realized how she would raise the money Sasha needed. She would become a prostitute.

At first the idea revolted her. But when she remembered Sasha's heroism she vowed to do it. If Sasha could sacrifice his very life for the Cause, she could certainly sacrifice her body for a night or two. The heroines she admired in Russian novels did no less. If she could become a capitalist for the Cause as she had done in Worcester, then surely she could become a prostitute for it. Sasha, with his endless insistence that the end justifies the means, would be proud of her if he knew.

With $5.00 she borrowed from a friend, Emma bought some high-heeled shoes, a pair of silk stockings, and fabric for making fancy underwear. She dressed herself up to look the part as well as she could. Then she joined the other streetwalkers on Fourteenth Street.

As a prostitute Emma was a total failure. However much she wanted to attract customers, she seemed instead to turn them away. It wasn't her looks, for she was a very pretty young woman with soft blonde hair and blue eyes and pert features; it was her manner. After several tries, she finally succeeded in capturing one man's interest. He took her to a bar and talked to her. After a little while he gave her $10.00 and told her to go home. "There is no way to be a prostitute without the knack," he told her. "You haven't got it, that's all."

Emma went home with the money and repaid her friend's loan. She still needed $15.00 more for Sasha. In desperation she wired her sister Helena in Rochester to send her $15.00, and when it came she sent it straight off to Sasha.

On Saturday, July 23, the day appointed for his act, Sasha went to Frick's office prepared to make the supreme sacrifice. He wore a new suit of clothes. He had a gun in one pocket, a dagger in another, and a dynamite capsule in his lapel lining, in case of emergency.

Rushing past a guard, Sasha pushed his way into Frick's office and found himself standing face to face with the "tyrant of Homestead" himself. As the two men faced each other, Sasha saw a look of terror cross Frick's face. "He understands," thought Sasha.

Sasha raised his revolver and aimed at Frick's head. He fired twice. Frick fell to the floor.

Someone rushed Sasha, and a carpenter who had been working in the building struck him on the head with a hammer. Sasha dropped his gun and fell.

From the floor where he lay dazed, he heard Frick's voice. "Not dead?" he thought with alarm. He took his dagger from his pocket. Somehow he managed to drag himself, with his assailants on top of him, over to where Frick lay, and he stabbed Frick three times in the leg. Frick struggled against him.

Suddenly a policeman rushed into the room. He was about to shoot Sasha when Frick commanded, "Don't shoot. Leave him to the law. But raise his head and let me see his face."

As the officer pulled Sasha's head back by the hair, the two men faced each other one last time. In his *Memoirs* Sasha describes the moment: "His face is ashen grey, the black beard is streaked with red and blood is oozing from his neck. For an instant a strange feeling, as of shame, comes over me; but the next moment I am filled with anger at the sentiment, so unworthy of a revolutionist." For a man who believed that the end always justifies the means, there was no room for shame, except the shame of failure.

When he was at last alone in jail, Sasha managed to slip into his mouth the dynamite capsule with which he had planned to kill himself after his trial. An officer discovered him chewing it and forced it from his mouth.

"What's this?" asked the officer, examining the capsule.

A look of supreme defiance spread across Sasha's face. "It's candy," he answered.

Sasha's attempt on Frick's life had done little but confuse the issues in the strike and reawaken a fear of anarchism across the country. His deed of propaganda worked more as propaganda against anarchism than for it. Frick was content to let the law dispose of Sasha; others were not so willing to let the matter rest. A cry went up to get the anarchists.

In Pittsburgh, two anarchist friends of Sasha who had nothing to do with the attack on Frick were arrested and convicted of conspiracy. A National Guardsman in Homestead was hung by his thumbs until he fainted, then court-martialed for treason, dishonorably discharged, and stripped of his right to vote—all because he had shouted, "Three cheers for the man who shot Frick!" In New York several prominent anarchists were arrested. The police, responding to newspaper demands, began to hunt for Emma, known to be Sasha's closest associate.

Emma and Fedya split up for safety. After the police raided the friends' apartment where she was staying, Emma had trouble finding work or a place to live. With her name daily in the papers, her friends were afraid to hide her. As soon as a landlord learned who she was, he would turn her away. She was forced for a while to sleep on the city trolleys and in the parks.

After days of searching, at last Emma found a room in a house where no questions were asked. It turned out to be a brothel, a house of prostitution. At first the discovery alarmed her. But soon she felt there was something almost fitting about her living there. Weren't prostitutes among the most oppressed victims of the capitalist system? They were so poor they had to sell their bodies, and for this they were abused and despised. Surely, thought Emma, she belonged among them. Within a week, all the women in the house had become her friends, and Emma was even able to earn her living sewing dresses for them.

Recovering rapidly from his wounds, Frick was soon back at his desk fighting the union. After the strikers had routed the Pinkertons, Frick convinced the governor to call out the Pennsylvania militia to "protect property" and "maintain order" in Homestead. The strikers could not be expected to take on the entire National Guard of the State of Pennsylvania. Once the troops were called, it was only a matter of time until Frick's plant was operating with nonunion labor. The union at Homestead was destroyed.

After Frick recovered, the police stopped hunting for Emma. While she waited for Sasha's trial, she began to write and eventually to speak in defense of his act as they had planned. But the public furor over Sasha's act made her job extremely difficult, for everyone reacted with horror and condemnation.

Now, it is possible to condemn an act of propaganda and at the same time sympathize with or admire the motive of the person who commits it. It is the motive—disinterested, selfless, altruistic—which is supposed to distinguish the propagandist from the ordinary criminal. The ordinary criminal commits a crime for per-

sonal benefit; the propagandist does so as a personal sacrifice. But even a justifiable act of protest or civil
disobedience is ineffective if it is widely misunderstood.
In Sasha's case, not only was his act immediately condemned by almost everyone, but his motive was almost
universally misunderstood as well. No one sympathized
with Sasha's motives because in America, where one
could make oneself heard by word or vote, there was
never any tradition or precedent for violent acts of
propaganda to make motives understandable. People either doubted that Sasha's act was selfless, or if they believed it they thought him a lunatic. The Homestead
strikers, for whom Sasha felt he was making his sacrifice,
repudiated the act immediately. Some people believed
Sasha must have held a personal grudge against Frick.
The rest saw his deed not as a selfless sacrifice, however
misguided, but as the irresponsible act of an anarchist
madman.

Emma was determined to use all her skill and eloquence to correct these misunderstandings. For this, she
counted on John Most to help her. More than any other
person in America, Most had always stood behind violent deeds of propaganda. He wrote pamphlets on
bomb making; his *Freiheit* often called for propaganda
by deed; he had even gone to prison for praising the assassination of the czar. But shortly after Sasha's attempt
on Frick's life, Most, just out of prison, reversed his position. Whether it was because of his old quarrel with
Emma and Sasha, or because he had a genuine change
of heart about the value of terrorism in America, no
one knew for sure. For whatever reason, Most turned

against Sasha. He published an article questioning the value of individual acts of propaganda. He even dared to suggest that Sasha had never really intended to kill Frick, that Frick had perhaps hired him to stage the attack.

Emma was incensed beyond endurance by Most's "betrayal." She answered his article with one of her own, denouncing him and challenging him to prove his insinuations against Sasha. Most never bothered to respond.

In Rochester, in a rage as violent as any of her father's, Emma had once physically attacked a woman for doubting the motives of the Haymarket martyrs. Now, in a comparable fury, she prepared to attack the man who doubted Sasha.

At Most's next lecture Emma took a seat in the front row. Hidden beneath her cloak she held a horsewhip. When Most rose to speak, Emma rose to confront him. One last time she demanded "proof" of his accusations against Sasha.

Mumbling something about a "hysterical woman," Most refused to answer her. Now Emma was satisfied. Standing defiantly before him, she pulled the horsewhip from under her cloak and leaped at Most, lashing him ferociously across his face and neck. When she was done, with one grand flourish she broke the whip across her knee and flung the pieces at his feet.

As quickly as she had appeared, she disappeared from the hall on Fedya's arm. It was all over before anyone in the stunned audience could interfere.

From that moment on until Most's death in 1906, the rupture in the American anarchist movement between

the followers of Most and the supporters of Emma and
Sasha was complete. The feud marked what one historian called "one of the most shameful chapters in anarchist history." Whatever else it did, it certainly increased Emma's notoriety and threw her more openly
than ever onto the anarchist stage. There was clearly no
one else like her in America.

8

Trials and Tribulations

We must learn, we Americans, to understand the guilty. They are in so many ways superior to the innocent.

—LINCOLN STEFFENS

Sasha's trial was another public farce, more cruel by far than Emma's sensational horsewhipping of Most. However terrible his crime, he deserved, like anyone else, a fair trial. He did not get one.

Sasha was not told the date of his trial until the very morning of the day it took place. When he entered the courtroom, the jury was already seated; he had been given no chance to exercise his right to question the jurors. Instead of being charged with the single crime he had committed, for which the maximum penalty was seven years of prison, he was charged with six separate crimes. The penalties could add up to twenty-two years. Any competent lawyer might have raised the necessary legal objections and made the proper motions for an appeal. But visionary Sasha had refused to have a lawyer. As an anarchist, he did not believe in the system of laws and lawyers. Instead, he chose to defend himself in court and use his trial to explain his crime to the public. As he put it, "The real question at issue is not a defense of myself, but rather the *explanation* of the deed. It is a mistake to believe *me* on trial. The actual defendant is Society."

In the days before his trial he had written in Russian a long and careful explanation of his deed. At the end of his brief trial, he was told he could address the court. When he began to read his prepared statement he was assigned an interpreter—so old and blind that he could hardly read the pages of Sasha's text. After only a few minutes of a painfully confusing word-by-word translation, the interpreter and Sasha were ordered by the judge to stop speaking, and the trial was declared over. Sasha was thereupon convicted, and sentenced to twenty-two years in prison.

That very day Emma had gone to Baltimore to deliver another speech in Sasha's defense. Just as she was mounting the platform to begin, someone handed her a telegram. It announced Sasha's sentence. She read it in disbelief. Twenty-two years instead of seven, and for a crime of which she was equally guilty. Frick was alive, and Sasha's act had gone totally misunderstood. A twenty-two-year sacrifice for nothing! She staggered to a chair.

When she recovered from the initial shock, Emma walked out onto the platform and began to speak about Sasha's sentence. It was an outraged, inspired speech. Her words were so impassioned that the audience rose together demanding vengeance. As soon as the shouting started, police burst into the hall and arrested Emma.

Two days later she was back in New York, sick with grief and guilt. Sasha at age twenty-two had begun to serve a prison sentence that would consume the central years of his life, while Emma, as guilty as he, had been dismissed from jail with the simple order never again to return to Baltimore.

Though the prospects of succeeding were bleak, Emma and Fedya gave all their energy to working for Sasha's early release. They wrote leaflets, organized mass meetings, and hired lawyers to file appeals and petition for a pardon. Emma worked ten and even twelve hours a day at her sewing machine to finance their campaign and to keep them alive. Sasha's rare letters were gloomy, and Emma's own letters to him left her dissatisfied. Once, by pretending to be Sasha's sister, Emma managed to visit him in prison. He even passed a secret message to her in a tiny capsule that he slipped into her mouth when they kissed. But one of the guards finally recognized her. After a terrible scene it was clear she would not be permitted to visit him again.

At one of the many meetings Emma organized to raise support for Sasha, she met an Austrian anarchist with the unlikely name of Edward Brady. He showed a special sympathy for Sasha that drew Emma to him. He had himself just finished serving a ten-year prison term in Austria for publishing illegal anarchist literature. Joining in all of Emma's efforts for Sasha's release, he, Emma, and Fedya quickly became close friends.

Ed Brady was the most scholarly person Emma had ever known. His knowledge, unlike John Most's, ranged far beyond politics and economics. He had an immense love of language and literature—English, French, German—that he shared eagerly with Emma. He was as ardent a teacher as she was a pupil. It was not surprising that they began to love each other.

That year after the Homestead strike was a disaster for American workers. It started with a great stock-market panic in 1893 that went on to become an economic depression lasting for four gloomy years. In the summer of 1893 four million workers were out of jobs. Their families were turned out of their homes when they couldn't pay the rent, and they had nothing to eat. The government provided almost no relief for them. They stayed hungry and sang radical songs.

Oh why don't you work like other men do?
How in hell can I work when there's no work to do?

The anarchists immediately began agitating among the unemployed. They tried to convince them that in a different kind of society there would be no unemployment. With Ed Brady to back her, Emma feverishly began collecting and distributing food, addressing rallies, and organizing relief committees. When the unemployed of New York City planned a mass demonstration in Union Square, Emma was on hand to help from the start. She believed the people had a right to jobs and a right to food and that the only way for them to get them was to demonstrate and demand them.

On the day of the demonstration four thousand people gathered to march on Union Square. Leading the march were the unemployed women, and at the head of the women was Emma. She was carrying a bright red flag, the banner of labor and the symbol of revolution.

When everyone had squeezed into Union Square the speeches began. One man spoke of the need for the government to create jobs; another demanded that the government distribute food. Their demands seemed absurd to Emma. Didn't everyone know that the state legislature had already refused to create more than token jobs or distribute more than token amounts of food? Emma was scheduled to speak last. She would tell the jobless how useless it was to petition the government; she would tell them that their only hope was to take direct action.

At last it was Emma's turn. Everyone began shouting, "Emma Goldman, Emma Goldman, Emma Goldman!"

She stepped forward, her temples throbbing and her knees trembling, and began one of those magically moving speeches for which she had already grown famous on the East Coast. She told the mob how absurd it was to expect relief from the government, the very "pillar of capitalism."

"Do you not see the stupidity of asking relief from Albany with immense wealth within a stone's throw from here?" She told them they had a right to share in their rich neighbor's bread if they themselves had none. Even the eminent Cardinal Manning had said as much. "Your neighbors," Emma said, "will go on robbing you, your children, and your children's children, unless you wake up, unless you become daring enough to demand your rights. Well, then, demonstrate before the palaces of the rich, demand work. If they do not give you work, demand bread. If they deny you both, take bread. It is your sacred right!"

The crowd received the speech with deafening applause. The next day the newspapers reported that "Red Emma" had urged the mob to revolution. The police, some said, must stop her.

Emma quickly left New York for Philadelphia. The police were right behind her. As she was about to deliver another speech, she was arrested and thrown into a Philadelphia jail until she could be transferred to New York. The charge was inciting to riot in Union Square, though no riot had ever occurred.

She was taken back to New York on the train by a Detective Jacobs of the New York City Police. He was extremely nice to her. He ordered a good dinner to be served her in her car. Over dinner he talked to her at length, complimenting her on her youth and her brilliance. How sorry he was, he said, that her talent would all be wasted in prison.

Emma was suspicious. "What's on your mind?" she asked.

Detective Jacobs came straight to the point. The chief of police in New York would drop the charges against her and pay her a handsome fee, he said, if she would work with him. All she would have to do was report now and then on the activities of the radicals she knew.

Emma couldn't believe it. Was this man really trying to bribe her to become a police spy? Could he really think she would betray her friends and herself? She snatched up a glass of ice water from her dinner tray and dashed it in Detective Jacobs' face, oblivious of his power to harm her. "I'll take prison for life," she said contemptuously, "but no one will ever buy me!"

The next morning she was taken before the chief of police himself. He was enraged that she had refused his offer. He threatened to have her locked away for years. But Emma was someone who simply did not scare. Instead, she made her own threats, promising to expose to the whole country the corruption of the New York City Police Department.

The chief picked up a chair to throw at her—then changed his mind. Clearly, this small, vigorous woman was impervious to threats. She would have to be handled in some other way. He called a guard to return her to her cell in the city jail known as the Tombs. There she waited to be bailed out by her friends.

While she waited in the Tombs, a well-known reporter of the day, Nellie Bly, came to interview her. Emma's case was so sensational that the interview appeared on the front page of the New York *World*. As usual with articles about anarchists, the interview centered on the aspects of anarchism most outrageous and fascinating to the public—the anarchists' rejection of society's pet institutions of religion, the State, marriage. "I believe in the marriage of the affections. That is the only true marriage," Emma replied plainly to a question, and the next day all New York twittered. The reporter touched on other things: on love and cleanliness, on terrorism and revolution. To her surprise, Nellie Bly found Emma no wild terrorist or seductress but a pretty, intelligent woman without a trace of frivolity. "She sacrifices her looks for books," wrote Nellie Bly, amazed. She reported Emma to be an honest and dedicated woman whose opinions, if they were strange or shocking, were at least absolutely sincere.

Sincerely held or not, it was chiefly for her shocking opinions that she was convicted at her trial. The prosecuting attorney found her views no less titillating than did the newspaper-reading public. He questioned her repeatedly about them. He seemed to think that if the jury found Emma's opinions wicked enough they would find her guilty too—whether or not her Union Square speech had incited anyone to riot.

Unlike Sasha, Emma accepted the services of a lawyer. An ex-mayor of New York, her lawyer, A. Oakey Hall, took the case free of charge. He expected to make a comeback into politics through the publicity the case would bring him. But not even he could keep questions about Emma's beliefs out of the trial, though such questions were clearly out of order.

The chief witness against Emma was the very Detective Jacobs who had tried to bribe her on the train from Philadelphia. He testified that he had written down Emma's Union Square speech word for word (though he was no stenographer) and that in it she had urged the crowd to riot. When even the judge announced before the jury that Emma was a "dangerous woman in her doctrines," no one doubted that the jury would find her guilty. Emma told a reporter that she would surely get a year of prison, "not because my offense deserves it, but because I am an anarchist."

She predicted her sentence correctly. After the jury pronounced her guilty, the judge sentenced her to one year in Blackwell's Island Penitentiary. Surrounded by police and reporters, she was taken from the court directly to the prison boat bound for Blackwell's Island.

Emma was heading for a grim year, perhaps the grimmest of her life. Yet she managed to appear brave and in high spirits. "Don't write any more lies than you can help," she called jovially back to the reporters as she boarded the prison boat.

Everyone laughed. "You can't squelch that kid," said one admiring reporter over and over. "You just can't squelch that kid."

Emma Goldman at seventeen, in 1886.

The Goldman family, St. Petersburg, 1882. Left to right: Emma, standing; Helena, seated, with Morris on her lap; Taube; Herman; Abraham.

Alexander Berkman at twenty-one, in 1892.

Henry Clay Frick.

A police photograph of Emma Goldman, taken when she was arrested after the assassination of McKinley in 1901.

The "Home for Lost Dogs," 210 East Thirteenth Street, as it looks today. (MARTIN SHULMAN)

EMMA GOLDMAN'S

FIVE SUNDAY NIGHT LECTURES

AT 43 EAST 22nd STREET

NEW YORK

AUTHOR:
ANARCHISM AND OTHER ESSAYS
PUBLISHER OF **MOTHER EARTH MAGAZINE**

Nov. 19. Communism, the most practical Basis for Society.

Nov. 26. Mary Wollstoncraft the pioneer of modern womanhood.

Dec. 3. Socialism caught in the political trap.

Dec. 10. Sex, the great element of creative work.

Dec. 17. Farewell lecture.

Meetings will begin at 8 P. M.   Questions and Discussion

Admission 25c.   *Tickets on sale at* **Mother Earth, 55 W. 28th St.**

   Sachs & Steinfeld, Union Printers. 12 Jefferson St.

An announcement for a series of lectures by Emma Goldman

Emma Goldman.

Ben Reitman, the "King of the Hobos."

Alexander Berkman speaking in Union Square, 1914.

(BROWN BROTHERS)

Alexander Berkman addressing a meeting of the Industrial Workers of the World.

(BROWN BROTHERS)

Alexander Berkman arrested for opposing the draft. New York, 1917. (BROWN BROTHERS)

An immigration officer checks Emma Goldman's passport as she returns to the United States for a ninety-day lecture tour after fifteen years of exile. February 1, 1934.

(UNITED PRESS INTERNATIONAL PHOTO)

Emma Goldman, just returned from Spain, addresses a London meeting on the role of trade unions in the Spanish Civil War. January 20, 1937. (WIDE WORLD PHOTOS)

9

School Behind Bars

I had evolved a crash program which I would immediately activate whenever I was placed in solitary: stock up on books and read, read, read.
—ELDRIDGE CLEAVER

For most people who go to jail, prison is an interruption of their lives. For Emma, whose life had long consisted in working among society's victims, prison was simply a new stage on which to act out her ideals. In prison she was thrown in among the lowest and most oppressed of society's discards—"derelicts on the social dungheap," as she described them. They had been declared criminals, like Emma herself, according to laws Emma regarded as unacceptable. They had been stripped of the last glimmerings of their personal liberty by the force of the State. Prison was a better place than many for Emma to do her work.

At first most of the inmates feared and mistrusted her. Wasn't she a confessed anarchist and atheist? Believing in neither government nor God, wasn't she a freak? On Sundays after chapel, when the prisoners were permitted to visit each other's cells for an hour, no one dared to visit Emma.

Then things began to change. Shortly after she arrived at Blackwell's Island, Emma was put in charge of the prison sewing shop. When she was told she would have to get more work out of the women under her, she refused outright. She said she would prefer to be sent to the dreaded dungeon than be a slave driver.

News of the incident traveled rapidly through the prison. On the following Sunday after chapel, every woman in Emma's tier of cells paid her a visit and thanked her. Before long they were vying with each other to do her favors and gain her confidence, and soon they became her friends.

Once when she had lived in the brothel, Emma's integrity and warmth had won her the love of the prostitutes with whom she lived. Now the prisoners on Blackwell's Island began to respect and love her too. "It is so easy to get their love. The least bit of kindness moves them," she later wrote to a friend from prison. "But what can one do for them? . . . The harm, the irreparable harm is done by the very fact that human beings are locked up [and] robbed of their identity."

Almost everyone who came in contact with Emma was somehow moved by her. Her absolute refusal to compromise her principles brought her admiration not only from the inmates, but from the prison authorities. She was in many ways the least cooperative of prisoners, always ready to denounce the corruption rampant in prison. She could fold her arms across her chest and, glowering fiercely, say "no!" to any order that went against her notions. But she was so generous and principled and trustworthy that the warden himself came to regard her as a "model prisoner."

The head matron was an exception. Once she asked Emma to translate for her some Russian letters one of the prisoners had written. Emma refused. She would not even *read* a private letter, she said, let alone translate one for the authorities. Furious, the head matron ordered her to the dungeon.

The dungeon was a tiny, damp, windowless cell where prisoners were put in solitary confinement. To be sent there was the worst punishment in prison. People went mad in the dungeon. For Emma, however, the dungeon was not much different from her own cell. Like many of the guards, the dungeon guard loved and trusted Emma. Knowing she would never try to escape, the guard left the cell door ajar all night to allow Emma a bit of light and air, and she gave her a chair, a blanket, and coffee to have until morning.

It was the same story when Emma fell ill and was sent to the infirmary for a month. The chief doctor, Dr. White, found her so helpful to the other patients that he asked her to stay on and run the sixteen-bed ward for him. He could easily teach her the rudiments of nursing, he said. Emma accepted the offer eagerly. The sick inmates needed her as much as anyone outside prison ever had. In a short time she became such an efficient and diligent nurse that after her year of prison was up she would continue as a practical nurse in Dr. White's office.

Altogether, prison was less a punishment for Emma than an education. When she entered prison, though she didn't know it, she was entering one of the most elite schools in the world. Many social idealists and revolutionaries before and after her, from Bakunin to Malcolm X, have claimed that they received the most valuable part of their educations in the privacy of their prison cells. There on Blackwell's Island, amid the worst squalor and degradation she had yet lived through, she faced her deepest doubts and tested her strengths.

"For people with ideals," Ed Brady had told her, "prison is the best school." When he had been in prison he had read incessantly in order to keep himself from going mad, and he had emerged the most scholarly person Emma had ever known. In prison there was time to read and think and reflect. After the endless lineups, inspections, and degrading marches between her damp cell and the workroom or infirmary; between the meager, tasteless meals and the nightly locking up, Emma read. She read volume after volume of literature and philosophy, history and poetry. Some of the books she got from Ed, some from the prison library. She cultivated the English language and studied about America.

But more valuable to her education than all the books she read was the certainty she gained about her own ideas and capabilities. Prison strengthened her convictions, as it had those of so many other idealists before her. Bakunin had described his own strengthening in a letter to his sister Tatiana:

> Prison has been good for me. It has given me leisure and the habit of reflection, it has, so to speak, consolidated my spirit. But it has changed none of my old sentiments; on the contrary, it has made them more ardent, more absolute than ever, and henceforward all that remains to me of life can be summed up in one word: liberty.

The same thing happened to Emma. Before entering prison, she had often seen the world through the eyes of her closest friends, like Sasha and John Most and Ed Brady. In prison she learned to think things out for herself. She learned to trust her own feelings and conclusions. She discovered in prison that she was strong enough to stand absolutely alone—against the whole world, if need be—to live her life without compromise. That knowledge was the crown of her education.

She had always been exceedingly brave. Now, after surviving the worst indignities of prison life and losing all her liberty, she knew there was nothing left in the world for her to fear. No threat would ever be able to touch her. "The State of New York could have rendered me no greater service," she wrote, "than by sending me to Blackwell's Island Penitentiary!"

10

Into the World

I do not know how one would set about destroy-ing Emma, except by frequent charges of high explosive, carried on for a very long time; and I think that the dust of the thus disintegrated Emma, borne through the air, would still con-tinue to utter the truth, the whole truth, and nothing but the truth.

—REBECCA WEST

On her release from prison, Emma found that the pub-licity connected with her sensational trial and sentence had made her something of a national celebrity. Before her imprisonment, her work had been conducted mainly among other immigrants. Now native Amer-icans—not only radicals, but reformers and celebrity-hunters—seemed to be taking her up. Daily she re-ceived invitations to luncheons and dinners, meetings and teas. She was glad to be pursued by Americans. Believing that only the native people of a land can bring about real, fundamental change in it, she felt it was they whom she needed most of all to reach. In prison she had studied American literature and the English language. But had she learned them well enough to lecture in English? She didn't know. The only way to find out was to try it.

She moved into an apartment on Eleventh Street in New York's Greenwich Village with Ed Brady. Fedya had taken a job out of town. Between the money Ed earned selling insurance, the money Fedya sent Emma every week out of his salary, and the money she was able to earn herself as a practical nurse, she could soon afford to plunge back into the anarchist movement. Within months of her release from prison, she was back on the lecture platform, publicizing anarchism and campaigning for Sasha's release. And occasionally she tried out her English.

It worried Emma that she couldn't support herself completely. Practical nurses earned little more than servants. If she wanted to live by nursing, she knew she would have to have training and a nursing degree.

Ed had always spoken of his native Vienna as a center of learning and culture. The most advanced medical ideas, he said, were being taught there. Now he and Fedya, with Sasha's encouragement, proposed to send Emma to Vienna to study nursing. At the same time she could stop in London, where many European radicals lived in exile, and meet the "great people" of European anarchism.

So it happened that in August 1895, less than ten years after she had first journeyed to America, Emma sailed back across the ocean to Europe. In London the

great Peter Kropotkin himself warmly received the
pretty sister from America. The Italian Enrico Malatesta and the French Louise Michel became her friends.
They were the legendary leaders of European anarchism. As Emma delivered speech after speech to London audiences, her fame spread and the crowd of her
admirers swelled. By the time she was ready to leave
London for Vienna, the twenty-six-year-old Emma had
built a solid reputation among the many European
social-revolutionaries living in London.

London was one of the few places in Europe at the
time where free speech and dissent were permitted. Vienna was quite another sort of place. In repressive Vienna Emma did not even dare to study nursing under
her own name. Instead, she registered for classes in
nursing and midwifery as Mrs. E. G. Brady, taking di-
plomas in both at the end of the year. She was able to
attend the lectures of Sigmund Freud. His startling
ideas about the role of sex in human psychology influenced her own already radical notions. She fell under
the spell of the writings of Friedrich Nietzsche, the op-
eras of Richard Wagner, and the works of the new European playwrights like Ibsen and Hauptmann. She was
in love with what was called the "new literature," giddy
over her new learning. Instead of sleeping at night, she
attended the opera and the theater as often as she could,
or she stayed up very late to read her precious books. It
seemed that there was no end to her passion for learning. The extra hundred dollars Fedya sent her at the
end of her trip to spend on clothes, she spent instead on
books. These she carried in a suitcase aboard her home-

bound ship, rather than send them through as baggage in the ship's hold. They were too precious to her to risk losing.

She returned to America more worldly and confident than when she had left. Despite her accent, she resolved to lecture as often as she could in English, spreading the message of anarchism among Americans. At first she was timid about speaking English, but as she became more practiced she began to move American audiences as readily as she had moved those that spoke Yiddish, Russian, or German. For a time, while she practiced her English, she also practiced her nursing, delivering babies as well as speeches to the wretched women of New York's teeming Lower East Side slums.

Finally she felt herself ready. Half eager, half hesitant, she set off on her first great cross-country tour, lecturing in English. It was the first of many, and it was a smashing success.

Around the turn of the century oratory was a powerful art in America. Speechmaking was big business. Famous speakers sometimes earned as much as $1,000 for a single lecture. The railroads provided fast, easy transportation from city to city for popular speakers, and the growing cities provided eager audiences. The orator could become more than a celebrity. Like today's television stars, an orator could mold opinion, whether speaking from the platform, the pulpit, or the stump. Millions of people flocked to lecture halls, sometimes traveling long distances to catch a celebrated speaker.

Already notorious as an anarchist, Red Emma became one of the "star performers" of the continent. She toured the country almost continually between 1896 and 1899. She attracted enormous audiences everywhere she went, delivering a dozen carefully prepared lectures on subjects ranging from Anarchism to Sex and Marriage. There was nothing she was afraid to talk about and no audience she was afraid to take on. She had a flair for the dramatic and a sense of timing that made her a natural star. She delighted in deflating anyone's self-importance and in exposing pomposity. "I suppose I shall remain all my life incurably giddy," she once said. Whatever she did made good copy, and everywhere she went she attracted reporters and the curious as well as people interested in her ideas.

Not infrequently she was arrested in the middle of a speech. But a night in jail was a small price to pay for the added publicity the newspapers would give her. She always carried a book with her to read in jail, in case she was arrested. In her profession, she once told a friend, she had to be able "to accept the station-house or a hotel with the same grace."

She never charged admission to her lectures if she could help it, since it was the poor she most wanted to reach. She supported her tours from her own resources, even for a time becoming a traveling salesman for one of Ed's inventions.

Her courage to speak despite harassment, her audacious style, and most of all her magical way with words, brought her many admirers. The newspapers denounced her, but at the same time they delighted in her antics. Many reformers who deplored her radical views rushed to defend her freedom to speak. For many

Americans, however, her legendary speaking power seemed to be a gift of the devil, and her sole purpose to move people to mad acts of violence and evil. Everyone had an opinion about Red Emma. Whether she was feared or admired, wherever she went crowds of people flocked to hear and heckle her. It was all the same to Emma: she could hold a hostile audience as easily as a friendly one. "The more opposition I encountered," she boasted, "the more I was in my element."

In Providence she was arrested during a speech and locked up for the night "just because you're Emma Goldman," explained the sergeant. In St. Louis the police were so afraid of her that they broke up a large public meeting as soon as she began to address it, sending everyone scampering.

In Detroit a minister was run out of town because of her. The minister, impressed by a speech he had heard her deliver, invited her to address his parishioners from his pulpit. Newspaper headlines warned: "Congregational Church to be turned into Hotbed of Anarchy and Free Love." Emma vowed to stick strictly to the announced topic of anarchism. But when several parishioners questioned her from the floor on her views of God and sex, she felt she had to answer honestly. "Blasphemy!" "Heretic!" "Sinner!" the congregation cried. In the ensuing scandal, the minister had to resign his post and move out of Detroit.

In San Jose, California, an angry audience of hecklers was so disruptive that Emma couldn't even get the meeting started. "Supposing one of you boys comes up here," she said in desperation, "and shows me how to keep the rest quiet until I have stated my side of the story. After that you can state yours." It worked. She delivered her speech uninterrupted and won over the mob. Not only did they listen; they gave her a huge ovation at the end.

And so it went, back and forth across the country. Emma was one of that handful of people who attract admirers and gain converts wherever they go. Roger Baldwin, for example, the tireless civil libertarian, was just one of the many people who fell under the spell of Emma's words. "Years ago, when I was a youngster just out of Harvard," recalls Baldwin,

> Emma Goldman came to town to lecture. I was asked to hear her. I was indignant at the suggestion that I could be interested in a woman firebrand reputed to be in favor of assassination, free love, revolution and atheism; but curiosity got me there. It was the eye-opener of my life. Never before had I heard such social passion, such courageous exposure of basic evils, such electric power behind words, such a sweeping challenge to all values I had been taught to hold highest. From that day forth I was her admirer.

Though Emma's style of speaking was provocative and inflammatory, she always came across as intensely earnest. Who could help admiring her courage? She was a "mountain of integrity," someone said; her idealism frequently inspired people to extravagant acts of devotion and generosity. During those traveling years she became the friend of many key American radicals, anarchist and nonanarchist alike. Many of them would remain her supporters for life.

Two wealthy admirers, Herman Miller and Carl Stone, whom Emma met lecturing in Detroit, even offered to make a childhood dream of hers come true. One evening she casually confessed to them that it was only lack of funds that had kept her from becoming a doctor. Instantly they offered to pay her way. They would send her to medical school in Switzerland, they said, and pay her a monthly allowance for five years while she studied.

Delighted with the offer, Emma had every reason to accept. She had finally separated from Ed Brady after seven years with him, and was free of ties to New York. Sasha's last appeal for a pardon had been turned down; now, planning a complicated escape from prison, he wanted her out of the country. That way, he said, she could avoid suspicion and he could join her abroad after he escaped. The first International Anarchist Congress was scheduled to be held in Paris the following year, coinciding with the great Paris Exposition of 1900. She could take time out from her studies in Switzerland to attend the Congress. A new century, a new profession. Why not? She accepted the offer of her friends.

Miller and Stone gave Emma a wardrobe of new clothes, a strange gold watch in the shape of a clam, money for a ticket on a London-bound ship, and enough extra money to carry her through the first few months abroad.

She arrived in England in dreary November. As she

delivered speech after speech, her fame spread. Never out of love for long, Emma soon met and fell in love with an exiled Czechoslovakian anarchist named Hippolyte Havel. He was a delicate, nervous man for whom she felt a strange fascination. He seemed to know everything and everyone in the European anarchist movement. Together Hippolyte and Emma joined the anarchist movement in England, and when the time came for Emma to go on to Paris, they went together.

Paris was the grandest place Emma had ever seen. The Exposition of 1900 was in full swing when they arrived. They wanted to take in everything. Paris was almost as rich in music and drama as Vienna had been, richer in art. And it was in Paris that anarchism had come alive in the preceding decades. In Paris the father of anarchism, Pierre-Joseph Proudhon, had issued his famous battle cry "Property is theft!" In Paris, during the Commune of 1871, men and women had rushed to the barricades to protect the city from its enemies as, for a brief moment in history, it lived under anarchist rule.

The International Anarchist Congress had been suppressed by the police and had gone underground. Meetings were held in secret. Emma attended them until at one she was refused permission to read a paper on sexual freedom for women. It was supposedly a freedom all anarchists believed in, but the French anarchists, fearing bad publicity, censored the paper anyway. Apparently, some freedoms were more important to them than others; as so often happened, women were expected to sacrifice their freedom first. Outraged, Emma resigned from the Congress.

She had the good luck to attend instead several secret meetings of the Neo-Malthusian Congress. This was an organization concerned with ways of preventing pregnancy in women and controlling the size of families. The whole subject of birth control was one in which Emma was especially interested. In her brief practice as a midwife in the slums of New York she had had to deliver many unwanted babies to women with families already too large for them to take care of. The women had begged Emma to tell them how to avoid becoming pregnant again. At the time, however, Emma didn't know herself. Now, at these Paris meetings, she learned various ways and means. She came away with precious information and a good supply of birth-control devices, called contraceptives. Of these she would eventually make much propaganda use.

Emma's Paris interlude with Hippolyte was interrupted by a letter from her benefactor, Carl Stone.

I thought it was understood when you left for Europe that you were going to Switzerland to study medicine. . . . I now learn that you are at your old propaganda and with a new lover. Surely you do not expect us to support you with either. I am interested only in E. G. the woman—her ideas have no meaning whatever to me. Please choose.

Emma's reply was in the next mail. Her independence was worth more to her than any amount of money. She wrote:

E. G. the woman and her ideas are inseparable. She does not exist for the amusement of upstarts, nor will she permit anybody to dictate to her. Keep your money.

Emma and Hippolyte had a little money left. They earned a little more by serving as guides to American tourists at the Exposition, and by cooking meals for friends. Then, suddenly, terrible news from home made them decide to leave Paris immediately. Sasha's escape plan, they learned, had been discovered, and Sasha had been banished to the dungeon. Frantic with worry, Emma and Hippolyte took the first available ship home.

Back in New York, Emma took up nursing and waited for news of Sasha. It was a long time before she heard anything. She felt helpless. Then one day she suddenly received two letters from him at once.

The one with the earlier date, written secretly, revealed that he had been in solitary confinement for more than a year. Emma knew that a week of solitary was considered the limit of human endurance. Sasha had somehow endured it for a whole year! The letter pierced her heart.

The second letter, dated two weeks later, told a different story. A new warden, hearing about Sasha's confinement, had had him returned to the general prison area. Sasha was allowed to have visitors for the first time in nine years. On top of that, a new law had reduced his sentence so that he had only five more years to serve. Now Emma was jubilant.

As soon as it could be arranged, she rushed to Pittsburgh to see him. Once again she disguised herself as his sister. Too tense to sit, she paced the visitors' room nervously. She wondered how Sasha would look and what she would say.

Finally a guard brought him in. Emma was appalled to see him. How vastly changed he was! He was battered and thin and half blind. She ran toward him with open, trembling arms. "Sasha!" she cried.

He couldn't answer her. His eyes, startled and tortured, said everything. He had been confined to the dungeon without human contact for so long he felt incapable of speech. It would take months of painful practice before words would again come easily to him, even words for Emma. They sat together in silence, absorbing each other with their eyes until the guard told them time was up.

Leaving Sasha, Emma remembered the impetuous act, the deed of propaganda, they had planned together those nine long years before. How differently she saw things now. Sasha, broken and half blind, had suffered away nine agonizing years of his precious life, and would still pay with five more. And for what? Had they been rash to try to kill Frick? Painfully Emma admitted they had been worse than rash. They had been wrong.

During her own imprisonment, Emma had thought deeply about the use of violence for propaganda. She had been stricken with doubts. How sad it seemed to her that the most principled, high-minded, selfless people—like the assassins of the czar or like Sasha himself—felt they must do "the very thing they abhorred most, destroy human life." She understood the impulse that led people to commit such extreme acts. It was their horror of the injustice and suffering everywhere around them. Everywhere they could see the organized violence of the State, the brutal violence of capitalism, which saturated the very atmosphere. How could the most sensitive idealists, moved to rage by organized brutality, help committing acts of violence in return? "Compared with the wholesale violence of capital and government," she wrote in an essay on "The Psychology of Political Violence," "political acts of violence are but a drop in the ocean." All her life she believed that "an act of political violence at the bottom is the culminating result of organized violence at the top."

But though she understood it, she no longer condoned it. Gradually, she stopped regarding acts of propaganda by deed as useful. She began to regard them instead as "deeds of misplaced protest." Little good and much suffering must come of them. She stopped believing that the end always justifies the means. She came to see that the means must influence the end, as surely as violence must breed more violence.

Every time a political assassination occurred, Emma felt the same regrets for the assassin's victim as for the assassin. When the empress of Austria and the king of Italy were killed in 1898 and 1900 by anarchists, Emma pleaded for the living assassins at the same time that she mourned the dead monarchs. All of them, killers and killed alike, seemed to her victims.

She had come a long way from the time when she and Sasha had been willing to experiment with bombs in a crowded tenement, risking innocent lives for the sake of what they happily called the Cause. Sasha's suffering in prison had taught her an unforgettable lesson. It was plain that Sasha was as much a victim of his act as Frick had been. No good had come of it. Both men were victims of all the violence and injustice in society itself.

There was only one way Emma knew to help Sasha and all the other tormented souls like him. There was only one way to make up for all his wasted years. That was to work harder than ever, without resort to violence, to promote the anarchist revolution. The State and capitalism must be overthrown. Society must be rid of the institutionalized violence and injustice that were the cause of the people's suffering and of Sasha's suffering. People's hearts and minds must be liberated. All society must be changed at the very roots and set free. Nothing less would do.

11

Superwitch

The old English offense of "imagining the king's death" has been formally revived by the American courts, and hundreds of men and women are in jail for committing it. . . . [It is] the crime known in America as "criminal anarchy."
—H. L. MENCKEN

Europe had celebrated the birth of the twentieth century with the great Paris Exposition of 1900. In 1901 the Americas celebrated with a fair of their own—the Pan-American Exposition at Buffalo, New York. The Buffalo fair was not nearly as grand as its Paris model, but it was important enough to merit a visit from the president of the United States himself.

On September 5—President's Day in Buffalo—100,000 people were on the fairgrounds wildly cheering President William McKinley. The president was delighted. He decided to hold a brief reception the following day where the people would be able to come close and shake hands with their friendly chief.

His secretary warned him that it would be unwise to stand face to face with so many strangers. Heads of State were always in danger of attack. Two United States presidents, Lincoln and Garfield, had been assassinated in the preceding half century, and before them President Andrew Jackson had barely escaped. At the present time there were rumors of international conspiracies and anarchist plots.

The president was not frightened. "No one would wish to hurt me," he said. And plans for his open reception went ahead.

At about four o'clock the following afternoon the doors of Buffalo's large Temple of Music were opened, and the public began to file in. President McKinley stood waiting in his black frock coat and white vest, surrounded by potted palms and police. Organ music filled the hall. The long line of celebrity seekers and well-wishers walked briskly through a double row of guards up to where the president stood smiling. Each one shook his hand in turn, then moved on out of the hall. The line moved quickly.

At seven minutes past four, a slim young man approached the president. His right hand was wrapped in a handkerchief intended to look like a bandage. He seemed quite ordinary; the guards did not suspect that his handkerchief concealed a revolver.

As the president reached forward to shake his hand, the young man fired two fast shots. A stain spread over the president's white vest. The bullets had struck his

chest and stomach and had set the young man's handkerchief aflame. Before he could fire again guards
knocked him to the floor. People screamed and fled.

While the bewildered president was helped to a
chair, soldiers piled on the assassin and began to beat
him. "Be easy with him, boys," called McKinley weakly.
But the request was useless. Guards raised the youth to
his feet only to knock him down again; soldiers beat
him with their rifles; someone tried to stab him with a
bayonet, someone else with a knife.

That night in his jail cell the young man wrote out in
longhand a crude confession: "I shot President McKinley because I done my duty." Asked if he were an anarchist, he answered, "Yes."

Eight days later the president died. With McKinley's
assassination the nation set off on another wild, brutal
rampage against anarchists.

The day the president was shot Emma was far from
Buffalo. She had been to the exposition, but that had
been weeks before. When the news came of the attack
on the president she was talking to a friend on a street-
corner in St. Louis. Her friend suggested that she might
be blamed for the tragedy. As America's best-known anarchist, Emma's name had been linked with almost
every political assassination of recent years. "It's fortu-
nate," said her friend, "that you are here and not in
Buffalo."

"Nonsense!" scoffed Emma. Why would anyone
blame her for the shooting? She did not wish the president dead. She did not approve of the assassination.

The next day in the local paper Emma read the following headlines:

ASSASSIN OF PRESIDENT MCKINLEY AN ANARCHIST.
CONFESSES TO HAVING BEEN INCITED BY EMMA GOLDMAN.
WOMAN ANARCHIST WANTED.

The assassination, the paper said, was another anarchist plot. Two hundred detectives had been sent out to track Emma down. Nine of her friends in Chicago, the paper said, had been arrested and were being held until she was found. Among them was Hippolyte Havel.

Emma stared at the paper, astonished at what she read. She knew that she and her friends were innocent of any plot against the president. She decided to go straight to Chicago and surrender.

Suddenly, as she read on, she came across a picture of the assassin, Leon Czolgosz. Though his name was unfamiliar, she recognized his face as that of a man she had indeed met before—on two brief occasions.

The first time she had seen him was several months before in Cleveland, where she had given a lecture on anarchism. He had been in the audience. Ironically, in that very lecture she had deplored the popular image of anarchists as bomb-throwing terrorists. She had declared quite plainly that she did not believe in violence, and that anarchism and violence did not have to go together. After the lecture, she remembered, the young man in the picture had introduced himself and asked her to recommend some books to read. He had introduced himself as Fred Neiman—the last name being the German word for "nobody." She remembered thinking he had a sensitive face.

The second time she had seen him was in Chicago a few days later. On that occasion they had exchanged only a few words. After that she had never seen or heard from him again.

How odd that the papers should now say he was her disciple or that she was his accomplice. Fred Nobody was so far from being Emma's disciple that her Chicago friends actually suspected he was a police spy. He claimed to be an anarchist, but he seemed to know suspiciously little about anarchism. Only weeks before, the Chicago anarchist journal *Free Society* had published a warning about him:

ATTENTION:

The attention of the comrades is called to another spy. . . . His demeanor is of the usual sort, pretending to be greatly interested in the Cause, asking for names, or soliciting aid for acts of contemplated violence. If this same individual makes his appearance elsewhere, the comrades are warned in advance and can act accordingly.

Detectives assigned to watch anarchist organizations in Cleveland, where the young man lived, did not recognize him. He did not belong to any known anarchist group. If he were, as he claimed, an anarchist, he was a lone one.

But the public was unwilling to believe that Czolgosz had acted alone. The press indicated that the assassination was an anarchist conspiracy, with Emma the instigator. A president had been killed; the nation was in a state of panic.

Back at the time of the Haymarket Affair a great fear of an anarchist peril had swept the country. Now, after the assassination of McKinley, the terror was revived, only this time it was even stronger. All across the land anarchists were hunted, arrested, beaten, persecuted. Their offices were raided, their papers confiscated. In Wyoming a man thought to be an anarchist was tarred and feathered. In Pittsburgh an anarchist was almost lynched. In New York City a mob had to be forcibly prevented from crossing the Hudson River and burning down the whole city of Paterson, New Jersey, where many anarchist workers lived.

When Emma finally turned herself over to the Chicago police, many people were relieved. Some even rejoiced. Czolgosz, the real assassin, was unknown and thought likely to be mad. His obscure life was not enough to pay for the murder of a president. Emma's was the life they wanted. Her very name brought terror to thousands of hysterical people. She was Red Emma the superwitch, who must burn. "Emma Goldman is a witch. True, she does not eat little children, but . . . she manufactures bombs and gambles in crowned heads" was the parody Emma herself wrote on the popular view of her. So strong was the feeling against her that her friends feared she would never emerge from jail alive.

She was charged with "conspiracy," a catchall crime, and locked up without bail in the very jail that had held Chicago's Haymarket martyrs. The police tried to force a confession from her. She was allowed no food or water or sleep during long hours of gruelling questioning under hot lights and fearful threats. A guard knocked out one of her teeth.

Far from frightening her, such tactics only made Emma more determined. However roughly she, in Chicago, or Czolgosz, in Buffalo, was grilled, the police were unable to come up with a single scrap of evidence against her. Though Czolgosz claimed to have been influenced by her teachings, he insisted to the end that it had been entirely his own idea to kill McKinley. "She didn't tell me to do it," he said. He had acted alone.

As usual, it was Emma's words, not her deeds, that outraged the public. She denied having had anything to do with the assassination; she even said she disapproved of it. But at the same time, she spoke up for the rights of the defenseless Czolgosz, and no one could believe she was not defending his act as well. "My compassion [is] with the living," she explained; "the dead no longer need it." But no one understood her explanation. Lawyers advised her that trying to save Czolgosz's life would be suicide for her. Any jury, they said, would see her pleas for his life as approval of his deed, and would likely judge her an accomplice. The lawyers' advice only disgusted Emma. She was the last person in the world to keep quiet for reasons of prudence. If she were the only person in America willing to speak up for Czolgosz, that seemed to her all the more reason to do so. What else was courage for?

The lawyers' predictions were never put to the test, for Emma's case never went to trial. Eventually the Chicago police released her. With no evidence against her, the Buffalo authorities could not extradite her, and the charges against her were dropped.

The newspapers that had reported her "capture" in huge, gaudy headlines buried the news of her release in the small print. An evil Emma was big news, but an innocent Emma was a bore. Though no jury condemned her, the press and the public did.

Emma set to work after her release to rally support for Czolgosz's defense, but almost no one was willing to help her. Not one landlord in all New York City was willing to rent her a meeting hall in which to speak for him. Reformers concerned with civil rights ignored the violated rights of the friendless Czolgosz. No one protested the treatment he received. Even anarchists remained silent.

Czolgosz was brought to trial as quickly as possible. At the trial, not one shred of evidence was offered to show that he had been aided or influenced by anyone. No anarchist conspiracy could be uncovered. Everything indicated that Czolgosz had acted completely on his own. Yet the nation panicked as though a huge, dangerous conspiracy had been disclosed. "Judging by the press," wrote Emma, "I was sure that it was the people of the United States and not Czolgosz that had gone mad." A psychiatrist who studied the case and attended the trial wrote of it: "I really do not think in all my experience that I have ever seen such a travesty of justice." The lawyers for Czolgosz's defense, assigned by the court, did not call a single witness to testify in his behalf. In their summary to the jury they simply eulogized the dead McKinley. After he was electrocuted, Czolgosz's corpse was destroyed by acid, as though its very presence in the ground could contaminate the land.

Long after her release, Emma was still feared and hated as a "murderer." Despite her unchallenged innocence, she became a complete outcast. No one would rent her a room. She was screamed at and cursed in the street. Luckily, a prostitute who had once been her patient let Emma stay in her room while she herself went to live with a friend. Emma's relatives in Rochester were persecuted. Her father was excommunicated from his synagogue. Her name, used to frighten small children, became legendary: Emma Goldman, murderer and superwitch. That she was innocent of the assassination and critical of violence escaped everyone's notice.

In his first message to Congress as the new president, Theodore Roosevelt warned the nation against the terrible dangers of anarchism. A number of senators proposed establishing a penal colony for anarchists "on some suitable island." Another senator said he would give $1,000 to get "one good shot at an anarchist." State after state hastily passed criminal-anarchy laws, making it a crime to advocate anarchism, though such laws violated the Bill of Rights.

Finally, in 1903, Congress passed the Anarchist Exclusion Act. That law ruled that no one could enter the United States "who disbelieves in or is opposed to all organized governments." With that bill, the cause of free speech in America was badly crippled. The long American tradition of welcoming all political refugees from other lands came to an end. From then on only people whose beliefs were acceptable to the government could enter the country.

For the first time in her life Emma felt that human ignorance and prejudice were so vast that they might never be overcome. She watched the reaction against radicals overtake the country like a disease. She blamed the radicals and reformers themselves as much as their enemies. Hadn't they, in their horror over McKinley's assassination, remained silent when the persecutions began on Czolgosz? He was denied the most basic constitutional protections, even a fair trial. That was the time to have protested. She was filled with disgust at humanity and contempt for her comrades' cowardice. She could not bear to speak to anyone. So great was her bitterness that for a time she withdrew completely from the movement.

Despised and ostracized by almost everyone, Emma quietly assumed the name of Miss E. G. Smith and went into seclusion. She attended no meetings. She saw none but her closest friends. She took inconspicuous jobs as a night nurse, and occasionally made dresses to order. Without the movement, Emma felt that her life had "lost its meaning" and that she had suffered a "spiritual death." Yet she was too bitter and depressed to return to the movement. Instead, she withdrew further and further into herself.

Years later she tried to explain that spiritual crisis. "The self-assurance with which I had always proclaimed that I could stand alone had deserted me," she wrote. "I had not been able to bear being repudiated and shunned; I could not brave defeat." It was easily the worst defeat of her life.

The persecutions of radicals continued, with or without Emma to fight them. One day Emma read in the newspaper about a new wave of bloody riots and pogroms in Russia. Many people were being killed by the czar's forces. The news shocked her out of her depression. The victims of repression in Russia needed her, and she was doing nothing for them. Suddenly she saw what a mistake she had made. By abandoning the movement she had lost touch with all that was important in her life. All because of her disgust with a mere handful of cowardly radicals, she had not only betrayed the people who needed her, but she had abandoned her ideals. The persecuted Russians and the hounded Americans needed her support more, not less, than before.

As though she were recovering from a long, severe illness, Emma slowly took up her work again. First she raised money for the new victims of the czar. Next, to the dismay of the police, she began agitating among Pennsylvania's striking coal miners. Finally, in 1904, she organized a test-case of the 1903 Anarchist Exclusion Act.

Emma had arranged an American lecture tour for the renowned British anarchist labor leader John Turner. The United States government was using the Anarchist Exclusion Act to try to deport him. When immigration officials arrested Turner on the platform of a crowded auditorium, Emma prevented a riot by calming the angry audience. A violent confrontation with the government over Turner would accomplish nothing, she said. A court fight of the case instead might make valuable propaganda.

Turner agreed to stay in America for the fight, and Emma went to work. As E. G. Smith, she organized the Free Speech League to spread the word. Branches of the League sprang up all across the country, uniting diverse reform and radical groups. It amused Emma that many of the most prominent members would never have joined if they had known that Red Emma the anarchist was behind it. They might not have exercised their right to free speech if she had exercised hers. The League was originally established to protect Americans from the repressive legislation enacted after McKinley's assassination. Eventually, however, it came to serve a much broader purpose.

When the Turner case finally reached the Supreme Court, not even Clarence Darrow, the most accomplished lawyer in America, could win it. In the end, the court upheld the Anarchist Exclusion Act, as Emma had all along expected. But though the fight was lost, it brought important issues into the open and drew many frightened reformers and radicals back into the libertarian movement.

By the time the case was closed and Turner had departed, Emma, through her work, had gradually become well again.

12

A Home for Lost Dogs

Emma Goldman does not merely preach the new philosophy; she also persists in living it,—and that is the one supreme, unforgivable crime.
—HIPPOLYTE HAVEL

With President McKinley, America had buried the nineteenth century. The twentieth century, and its first United States president, Theodore Roosevelt, brought a new spirit to the land. It was the spirit of progress, reform, and modernity. Telephones, telegraphs, automobiles, electric lights, suddenly began to be commonplace, giving the new era a special look and sound and feel. A new gusto and vitality stirred the nation. Everything seemed possible. Shouting exuberantly "I feel like a bull moose!" President Roosevelt proclaimed the spirit of the new era.

In the early decades of the century the word "new" itself was used for everything. Preachers preached a New Theology. The New Immigrants were crowding into the cities. Politics brought a New Nationalism and, later, a New Freedom. Newly launched magazines sported names like the *New Republic* and the *New Democracy*. In the salons of the new "bohemian" sections of the larger cities, the New Drama, New Poetry, New Criticism, and New Painting were discussed and practiced by artists, writers, and intellectuals. The "Progressive Era" was underway.

In 1903, as the public furor over Emma began to subside, she moved to a small cold-water flat at 210 East Thirteenth Street. There she would live for a decade, right in the thick of New York's sparkling Greenwich Village, where the new, heady spirit was fomenting. In those years in Greenwich Village "leaped a new generation so dashingly alive," wrote Alfred Kazin, a historian of the period, "that it was ever afterward to think it had been a youth movement." Emma's apartment, tagged by a friend a "home for lost dogs," became one of the centers of the new spirit. "There was always someone sleeping in the front, someone who had stayed too late and lived too far away or who was too shaky on his feet and needed cold compresses or who had no home to go to," she wrote. It was a place where friends could drink coffee "black as the night, strong as the revolutionary ideal, sweet as love."

Only, for Emma, little that went on there seemed especially new. The twentieth century's New Woman, practicing the New Morality and demanding the right to vote, was less daring than Emma had been most of her life. The New Psychology of Sigmund Freud that everyone was suddenly discussing had been familiar to Emma since 1895, when she had attended Freud's lectures in Vienna. The New Drama of Shaw, Ibsen, and Strindberg Emma had discovered on her own back in 1895. In fact, it was Emma's lectures on modern drama, later published as *The Social Significance of the Modern Drama* (1914), that had helped to popularize the New Drama in America. Emma had always been so far in the vanguard that she seemed to one journalist to be "about eight thousand years ahead of her age." The only new things in her own life at the time were her alias, E. G. Smith; her "oasis in the desert" at Thirteenth Street; and a massage parlor she opened in 1905 to free her from her long hours of nursing.

In the summer of 1905 many of Emma's customers started leaving the city for the seashore. Emma decided to do the same. Her niece Stella, Lena's daughter, had moved to New York from Rochester that winter to join Emma in her home for lost dogs. Now Stella got a permit to camp on Hunter Island in Pelham Bay. As soon as the hot weather set in, Emma and Stella pitched their tents on the island and invited some friends to join them.

Before long they heard of the plight of the great Russian actor Paul Orleneff. Orleneff had been chased out of Russia the previous winter for performing forbidden plays. Penniless, he had fled to New York with his entire acting troupe and had begun performing on the Lower East Side. Though Emma had never met him, she had seen him perform many times that winter and thought him a genius. He was staging some of the very plays Emma had lectured on, as well as the Russian plays of Chekhov and Dostoyevsky. All soul and sensitivity, he easily fascinated American audiences. "A great artist," agreed the New York critics. His troupe, wrote one critic, displays "a higher order of acting than [Americans] are accustomed to." But because he played only in Russian, mainly to the poor immigrants of the Lower East Side, he could not raise enough money to live on, and he and his troupe were put out on the streets with nowhere to go.

Generous by nature and eager to help the stranded Russians, Emma sent a message to Orleneff, inviting him and all his actors to join her camp. Genius or no, in America he was another lost dog. There was always room, she said, to pitch one more tent.

Orleneff accepted gratefully. All through that summer of 1905, each night at the camp he would close his great melancholy eyes and play his balalaika. And around him, beside a huge bonfire, Emma, Stella, and the whole troupe of actors would fill the air with sweet Russian songs or talk of Russia and the revolution to come.

One night, after the singing was over and the campfire was dying out, Orleneff begged Emma to become his manager. He might receive fourteen curtain calls for a single performance, he lamented, but he couldn't make enough money to live on. Perhaps if Emma took charge his luck would change.

Emma agreed to do it. He was, she said, "a naïve unworldly creature" who needed a manager. She closed the massage parlor, and for the rest of that summer and the following winter she acted as Orleneff's interpreter and manager, accepting no salary.

Once in an interview Orleneff had said, "I believe in pain. I believe in unhappiness. I believe Russian literature has a soul because the Russian people are unhappy." Emma did not believe in unhappiness, but she did believe in the social significance of the new drama and the artistic genius of Orleneff. She threw herself into the job of managing his troupe with her usual ardor. As E. G. Smith she wrung large financial contributions from the rich, and arranged play readings and benefits among the Russian-Jewish poor. She managed to raise a fund of $16,000 for the actors. Rich society ladies, like Mrs. Astor and Mrs. Vanderbilt, invited Emma to their grand mansions and handed her their checks. They would have been scandalized to know that E. G. Smith the manager was really Emma Goldman the anarchist. But to Emma's impish delight, they never even suspected.

At last, finding himself after a year still unable to speak a word of English, Paul Orleneff decided to return to Russia. Before he left, he wanted to show his gratitude to Emma.

"Miss Emma," he said, "what would you most like to do if you had money?"

Emma didn't have to think long. "I would start a magazine," she answered—a radical magazine in English in which "young idealists could voice unpopular opinions."

Orleneff decided to stage a special performance to raise money for Emma's magazine. He would put his whole soul into it—"because you have done so much for me."

Emma wanted her magazine to be a platform for the new artists and the old idealists. She hoped it could unite revolutionary and artistic expression. Aside from advancing her own radical work, she wanted to keep it free from political dogma.

At first she had trouble finding a name for it. Then she hit on a name that seemed to her exactly right: *Mother Earth*. Mother Earth, source of life, "nourisher of man"—that was just what she hoped her magazine might be.

When Orleneff's special performance was over, enough money had been raised to publish the first issue. The living room at 210 East Thirteenth Street, which also served as dining room and bedroom, quickly became the *Mother Earth* office as well. If the little apartment, as Emma claimed, could always hold one more person, it could certainly make room for her magazine.

On March 1, 1906, one month before Orleneff returned to Russia, Volume One, Number One appeared. On the masthead was printed, simply:

> MOTHER EARTH
> Emma Goldman, Publisher
> 10¢ a copy; $1.00 per year

Between the covers was a rich selection of articles on anarchism and on patriotism, on love and on prudery. There were poems, book reviews, and news reports.

Emma herself wrote a wise article on freedom for women and many witty, biting comments on events. The tone throughout was serious but not grave, insistent but not righteous. It was a new tone—distinctly hers.

Altogether *Mother Earth* ran for twelve long years, monthly, with only an occasional lapse because of police interference. It lasted much longer than most radical journals. Before 1920, only two other American anarchist publications lasted ten years or more. *Mother Earth* was considered "a pioneer spokesman for radical thought in the twentieth century." Almost every American anarchist writer and many Europeans contributed to it. In its pages Russian literature was often translated for Americans. Peter Kropotkin was a frequent contributor. But overall, Emma's own broad range of interests in art and politics pervaded the journal. She called the magazine her "child," and over the next dozen years she devoted herself to it as lovingly as any mother could. A new phase of Emma's life began when *Mother Earth* joined the family at 210 East Thirteenth Street.

Two months after Emma's "child" was born, another event occurred that touched the center of her life. On May 18, 1906, after fourteen agonizing years of prison, Sasha was at last set free.

On the day she would always remember as "the happiest of my life," she waited for Sasha at the railroad station with an armful of roses. She recalled their last meeting on a train, the day Sasha had left her, determined to shoot Frick. That parting was the last time she had seen him free. He had said goodbye to his Sailor

Girl expecting never to return alive. And now he was coming back to resume his life with her where he had left it, fourteen years before.

The whistle blew and the train pulled in. Suddenly they were standing face to face, two free people. Sasha's face was deathly pale, his smile joyless and pained. As she hugged and kissed him, tears rose in Emma's eyes. She tried uselessly to choke them back. Overcome by feeling, Emma and Sasha were once again unable to speak to each other. Instead, they walked down the platform silently, clinging to each other's arms, the rest of the welcoming party following behind.

Emma took Sasha back with her to her little apartment—another lost dog come home. When they were finally alone together that night, Sasha broke into uncontrollable sobs. He tried to tell Emma how tormented he felt. He could not bear the walls of the room. He could not bear to be alone or to be among people. He almost wished he were dead.

Emma knew no way to comfort him. During the trying time after McKinley's assassination, a wealthy friend had deeded to Emma a small farm in the state of New York. It was to be her refuge, the friend had said —a place from which no one could chase her, whatever happened. Now she took Sasha there to nurse him.

In the country Sasha went for long walks in the woods and fields, but his mind remained in prison. The very branches of the trees were like prison guards, and he would jump at the murmur of the leaves. Gratefully he devoured the meals Emma cooked to build up his broken body, but nothing seemed to nourish his starved spirit. Something had happened to him—and to the world—during his long imprisonment, something he was unable to cope with. The world he had left fourteen years before as a youth of twenty-two was not the same world he was returning to now. It seemed to him that everything had changed: the movement, his friends, even Emma. In this strange, new, twentieth-century world he felt dull and useless. Emma seemed to him no longer the fierce idealist who had helped him plan to kill Frick. Life had mellowed his Sailor Girl. She was a mature and worldly woman now, involved in a busy life unknown to him. The changes in her irritated him; he criticized all her ideas. He began to feel himself a drag on her and to resent her help. Disappointed in every change he saw, Sasha was inconsolably sad. When he and Emma returned to New York City, he tried to kill himself.

Emma did not know how to help Sasha. Sometimes she thought he was better when she was away from him. But whatever pain they caused each other, Emma knew their lives were bound together forever. She knew she would always be at his side when he needed her.

That year Emma had begun making speeches again under her own name. The police, with a newly created Anarchist Squad, constantly harassed her. One night they broke up an anarchist meeting with particular brutality, clubbing and arresting many people. Emma was charged with criminal anarchy and taken to jail.

Though the charges against her were eventually dropped, her arrest had a surprising result. To Emma's joy, it lifted Sasha out of his depression and deposited him in fighting form back in the world.

"My resurrection has come!" he cried when he heard about the police raid. "There is work for me to do now!" He felt independent and useful again; he had a reason to live. The more the police hounded the anarchists, the tougher Sasha grew. Like Emma he thrived under attack. "The enemy is challenging, the struggle is going on," he wrote in his memoirs, "and I feel a great joy in my heart."

With Sasha back on his feet, Emma set off on a long speaking tour. It was her first cross-country tour in a decade. The madness that had swept the country after McKinley's death had apparently subsided, for Emma was once again in popular demand as a speaker. She left Sasha, who was in many ways a better writer than she, in charge of *Mother Earth* and the apartment.

With the help of Hippolyte Havel and others of their little group, Sasha managed *Mother Earth* very well. So well that Emma left it in his hands again the following summer when she sailed for Europe to attend the International Anarchist Congress in Amsterdam.

At the conference Emma took a leading part in all the proceedings. Her speeches demonstrated that Sasha's feeling about her had been correct. Her political ideas had indeed changed over the years. When she and Sasha had been young rebels together she had been rash in her actions and naïve in her principles. She had been too much a libertarian to bother with details of organizing for the revolution, too much an idealist to concern herself with the organization of the society to come. In 1897 she had told a reporter: "I do not bother about all the trifling details; all I want is freedom, perfect unrestricted liberty." Now, in 1907, she was no longer simply a passionate rebel devoted to perfect freedom, ready to commit isolated acts of rebellion for some vaguely pictured Cause. She was a builder of a movement. Like every builder, she knew that details matter and that organization counts. Whereas in America she was considered chiefly an eccentric individualist, in Europe she was gaining a reputation as an organizer. Elected chairman for the last day of the Congress, she left as something of an international leader.

Before sailing for home Emma stopped briefly in Paris, and then in London. In Paris her imagination caught fire when she visited the Beehive, a children's school. Run on the anarchist principle that children, like all people, must follow their fancy and be free, in the Beehive there were no rules, no texts, no formal lessons. The children themselves decided what to learn and how to learn it. How different it was from the schools she had gone to. How different from any school she had ever seen before! To Emma, the ordinary authoritarian public school of her day was a tool of government, a "barrack where the human mind is drilled and manipulated into submission to various social and moral spooks." In the Beehive she saw no authority or competition. Here instead were freedom and understanding and love. Like a colony of bees, in which each one works for the good of all, the Beehive children worked together. Impulsively, Emma vowed to start such a school in America—a "modern" school like the Beehive. She left Paris inspired.

In London, her last stop in Europe, Emma received several letters from American friends with a strange warning. The United States immigration authorities, the letters said, were planning to bar Emma's reentry into the United States. She must, urged the letters, sail quickly and quietly for home.

At first Emma chose to ignore the warnings. The Anarchist Exclusion Act applied only to aliens, and she was an American citizen through her marriage to Jacob Kershner. But when she discovered she was being shadowed wherever she went in London, she realized that the warnings of her friends had been sound. She had broken no law; agents must be following her movements to keep the Americans informed. She decided to return home via Canada.

Zigzagging all over London, ducking in and out of restaurants and bars, she managed to shake the detectives trailing her. She hid in the home of a friend for several days, then secretly made her way to Liverpool. There she boarded a ship bound for Montreal, Canada. From Montreal she went by night train to New York, and the next day, at long last, she was safely home among her friends in the little apartment on Thirteenth Street.

It was not until her first public appearance two weeks later that anyone was aware that Emma had slipped back into the country. She was tickled to have pulled off the stunt so smoothly. A reporter asked her how she had managed it. "Go ask the immigration authorities," she said with a snicker.

Several months later Emma daringly left the country again, to deliver some lectures in Canada. Again the authorities tried to prevent her return. At the border she was picked up for questioning, but this time she was prepared. She produced a copy of Jacob Kershner's citizenship papers—all that was needed at the time to establish her own citizenship. The officials had to let her go.

Having let her slip through their fingers twice, the officials were determined not to let her escape a third time. Carefully they laid plans to get her. The United States Attorney General himself ordered an investigation "into the citizenship of Emma Goldman," and assigned two special agents to the case. Since Emma was a citizen through Kershner, the government's plan was to discredit Kershner's citizenship somehow, and thereby discredit Emma's. Kershner himself had disappeared some years before, making the government's task all the easier.

After much poking around Rochester, the investigators discovered that Kershner might have been under twenty-one when he applied for citizenship back in 1884. If so, he had obtained his citizenship papers by "fraud." These findings were presented at a "trial" where neither Kershner nor Emma appeared to defend themselves. They were not even informed that a trial would be taking place.

The judge's verdict was for the government. Kershner was stripped of his citizenship, and with him Emma was stripped of hers. Though Emma's name was not mentioned in the proceedings, it was no secret that she was the one the government was after. One of the two special agents assigned to the case, Special Attorney P. S. Chambers, wrote a letter notifying the United States Attorney General of the outcome of the trial. In it, Emma's name stood out. "This is the suit," read the letter, "which was entered for the purpose of depriving Emma Goldman of her rights of citizenship." Once again Emma was an alien.

Without citizenship it was simply a matter of time until the government could get rid of her. If she were foolish enough to leave the country again, she could easily be kept from reentering. In court Emma had once been asked why she didn't leave the United States if she didn't like its laws. She had answered, "Where shall I go? Everywhere on earth the laws are against the poor, and they tell me I cannot go to heaven nor do I want to go there." From now on, she would no longer have a choice. If she strayed too far from home, she would be one lost dog never to return.

13

The Red Queen and the Hobo King

Are you going to hang him anyhow—and try him afterward?

—MARK TWAIN

Emma arrived at the railroad station in Chicago in 1908 only to be told that she might as well turn around and leave town. The police, said her friends, would never allow Emma Goldman to make a speech in the Windy City.

Another depression had devastated the country that year. Millions of unemployed were demonstrating in the streets of all the cities. Chicago's City Hall, instead of providing relief for the jobless, had tried to silence them, ordering the police to make raids, beat heads, and arrest their radical leaders. As usual, the anarchists were the first targets. Free speech was only for the "right" speakers.

Emma liked nothing better than a free-speech fight. She was more amused than alarmed to see "a powerful country moving heaven and hell to gag one little woman." Folding her arms imperiously across her chest, she said to her friends, "I will stay," and she went on into town.

The papers exploded with the news: that dangerous anarchist woman was back again. The house Emma stayed in was watched by detectives day and night. She was followed everywhere. The police threatened all the auditorium owners so that not a hall in all Chicago could be rented for her meeting.

Then all at once an offer of a hall came through. Dr. Ben L. Reitman, the "King of the Hobos," sent word to Emma that she would be more than welcome to use the hobos' meeting hall for her speech. It was just a vacant, rundown storefront in the flophouse district, but straightened up it might seat as many as 250 people.

Emma had heard of Ben Reitman, the Hobo King. He had been one of the arrested leaders of a demonstration of hobos and other unemployed the week before. Hobos were the lone migrant laborers who drifted around the country looking for work. In 1908 more than one third of the workers in all industries were unemployed; a half million of them were hobos. Rolling their belongings into a blanket slung over their backs, the hobos tramped alone from place to place on foot or hitched rides on freight trains, living in the open air on practically nothing. Radical and freedom-loving, many of them were members of the anarchist-inspired labor union called the International Workers of the World (IWW) and nicknamed the Wobblies. Like tramps and bums, hoboes were feared and despised by "respectable" people. The Hobo King, thought Emma, doctor or not, was not likely to be very respectable. She sent word back to the doctor that she was interested in discussing his kind offer of a meeting hall.

That afternoon a tall man with a mass of beautiful black curly hair called on Emma. His thick curls spilled out from under a large black cowboy hat that sat capriciously upon his head. His hair looked as though it hadn't been washed in a long time. Wearing a flowing silk tie and carrying a heavy cane, he looked wild and picturesque. He introduced himself as Dr. Ben Reitman.

"So *this* is the little lady, Emma Goldman. I have always wanted to know you," he said. His soft, deep voice passed over Emma like a shiver. It made her uncomfortable.

"I also wanted to meet you," she said, managing to seem composed. "I wanted to meet the 'curiosity' who believes enough in free speech to be willing to help Emma Goldman."

They started planning the meeting in the hobo hall, but Emma was so distracted she could hardly keep her mind on their conversation. This exotic man, with his great brown dreamy eyes and his full, sensuous mouth and his magnificent hair had put her on edge the moment he walked into the room. She must get control of herself, she thought. She tried concentrating on his hands, but they too began to fascinate her. Narrow and white, with nails that "seemed to be on strike against soap and water," they moved hypnotically. She couldn't take her eyes off them.

When at last Ben left, Emma felt as though she had fallen under a spell. She was restless and disturbed. She suspected she was falling in love.

Ben's hobos and Emma's anarchists went to work cleaning up the storefront. Emma announced her meeting to the papers. Benches were set up. The windows were covered with curtains. Everything was made ready.

On the day of the meeting, a building inspector visited the hall. "How many people do you expect?" he asked Ben.

"Fifty," said Ben. He gave a low number, expecting trouble.

The inspector looked around. "Nine," he said flatly. "That's all it's safe for." He smiled, satisfied there would be no meeting.

Not easily defeated, Emma and her friends decided to try one last trick. They would arrange a concert at the Workmen's Hall, and when the music was over, Emma would speak unannounced.

All went according to plan, except that the police had turned out at the concert. Emma managed to slip backstage unseen. The music began. The moment it stopped, Ben walked onto the platform. "A friend you all know will now address the gathering," he announced. Then Emma stepped forward.

As soon as her first words were out, police stormed

the stage and dragged her from the platform in full view of the concertgoers. The outraged audience began to push menacingly toward the stage. Fearing for everyone's safety, Emma pleaded with them to stay calm. "Walk out quietly!" she shouted as police shoved her roughly toward the exit.

The next day indignant letters poured into the newspaper offices protesting the police action. There were several angry editorials. Some papers said Emma had averted a riot. Shamefully people admitted that twenty years after the Haymarket Affair there was still no free speech in Chicago.

Quickly Emma organized a Chicago branch of the Free Speech League before she had to leave for her next engagement in Milwaukee. Every prominent radical in town enlisted. Before she left Emma made a special point of saying goodbye to the dashing doctor, Ben Reitman.

In Milwaukee Emma couldn't get Ben out of her head. She kept remembering his strange narrow white hands and his black curls and how he made her feel when he walked into the room. She felt "like a schoolgirl, in love for the first time." Finally, overcoming a million painful doubts, she wired him to join her in Milwaukee.

Ben went straight to Emma. From then on for many years, wherever Emma traveled Ben went with her.

Listening to Ben recite the story of his youth, Emma thought it sounded more like a story from a book than from life. "I was enthralled by this living embodiment of the types I had only known through books," she confessed; "I yearned to be in the arms of the man who came from a world so unlike mine."

Ben Reitman had grown up fatherless in a tough section of Chicago on the edge of the criminal underworld. As a little boy he had made his way running errands for the prostitutes and gamblers of his neighborhood. When he turned eleven, he packed a knapsack, left home, and took to the road. He was a dreamer and a wanderer. For years he tramped over the world, living on handouts and odd jobs. Then suddenly his life changed. While he was working as a janitor in a Chicago medical school in 1899, some professors urged him to enroll as a student. He became a doctor. But he continued to work chiefly among the "tramps, hobos, bums, dope fiends, whores, pimps, and other seared souls" who knew and loved and trusted him. Eventually the hobos chose him as their spokesman. They crowned him King of the Hobos.

The hobos didn't like Ben's association with Emma. They felt deserted and betrayed when they learned their leader was "hitting the road with Emma Goldman the Anarchist Queen." They called a special meeting to discuss it. Solemnly they stripped Ben of his crown and declared him no longer their king.

Emma's followers didn't like it either. They berated Emma for taking up with an ex-tramp who was not even an anarchist. Sasha called Ben a fraud, a charlatan. No one could understand how she could love someone they thought unworthy of her. When Ben began teaching a Sunday School class in the *Mother Earth* office, the comrades' disapproval turned to ridicule, and they laughed at Emma for allowing it.

But Emma and Ben loved each other and didn't much care what anyone said. It was a physical love so strong that all the hostility of all their friends could not destroy it for a decade.

It was true that Ben was at times capricious, irresponsible, and even dishonest. But Emma knew he had much to give to the movement. Not only did he love Emma with a passion as intense as her own, but natural showman that he was, Ben arranged the most successful tours of her entire career as her manager and "advance man." During the 1910 tour, for example, Emma spoke 120 times in thirty-seven cities in twenty-five states, including many places where anarchism had never before been discussed. Her audiences were vast, her meetings overflowing. Twenty-five thousand listeners paid, and many more were admitted free. Emma and Ben distributed 15,000 pamphlets. To Emma's horror, Ben did occasionally pocket some of the funds, and now and then he ran off for a night with another woman. Still, Emma told herself, the movement was ahead financially and she was ahead emotionally because of Ben. "Hobo will learn," she said.

In city after city Emma and Ben battled for free speech as they had done together in Chicago. The police would try to keep Emma from speaking—by scaring the hall owners into refusing her their halls, or by breaking up her meetings, or by arresting her. Then

Emma and Ben would organize the aroused public, sometimes forming a Free Speech League, to carry on the fight. In Boston, New Haven, New York, Philadelphia, Indianapolis, Seattle, it was the same story, endlessly repeated.

The outrage against free speech reached a ridiculous high in San Francisco. One Sunday afternoon Emma was giving her lecture on patriotism. In it she told how blind love of the State causes war, legalized murder, mass madness. It turned out to be one of those spellbinding speeches only Emma could give. Everyone sat silent and tense until the lecture was over, then exploded into an avalanche of applause. Among the people who rushed up to shake her hand after the speech was an army private named William Buwalda.

Buwalda had been a soldier for fifteen years; he had received a medal for "faithful service." He knew nothing at all about anarchism; he had been passing the hall where Emma was speaking and had gone in out of curiosity.

For that innocent public handshake, Buwalda was followed out by detectives, arrested, court-martialed, sentenced to five years of hard labor in Alcatraz, and dishonorably discharged from the army. His crime, said the general who presided at the trial, was "shaking hands with that dangerous anarchist woman."

Ten months later Buwalda was pardoned by President Roosevelt himself. But by the time he was released from Alcatraz he had done a lot of thinking. He sent his medal back to the army with a letter explaining that he had "no further use for such baubles. . . . Give it to some one who will appreciate it more than I do," he wrote, and joined the anarchist movement.

While Emma led the fight for freedom to speak indoors, the radical IWW labor union was leading a similar fight for free speech outdoors. Towns all over the West Coast were banning street meetings and outdoor speeches in an effort to stop the Wobblies from organizing workers. The bans were unconstitutional, and the Wobblies sent out a call to all "foot-loose rebels" to board the freight trains and "come at once to defend the Bill of Rights." Hobos with their packs on their backs would stream into this town or that to defy the ban, fill the jails, and test the law.

In 1912 street meetings were banned in San Diego, California. Not far away, in Los Angeles, Emma was lecturing. Hundreds of people protesting the ban in San Diego were arrested, but thousands more came singing into town to take their places.

> We're bound for San Diego, you better join us now.
> If they don't quit, you bet your life there'll be an awful row.
> We're coming by the hundreds, we'll be joined by hundreds more,
> So join at once and let them see the workers are all sore.

Prisoners in jail were mistreated. Local Vigilante Committees formed to terrorize the new arrivals. Some of them were beaten and tortured; one was even killed. Local newspapers whipped the Vigilantes on. The San Diego *Tribune* said in its March 4 editorial on the Free

Speech Crusaders: "Hanging is none too good for them. They would be much better dead, for they are absolutely useless in the human economy; they are the waste material of creation and should be drained off into the sewer of oblivion there to rot in cold obstruction like any other excrement."

In May, Emma and Ben took a train from Los Angeles to San Diego to join the fight. When they arrived, there was a crowd at the railroad station. Unobserved, Emma and Ben boarded a bus for their hotel. Suddenly a woman shouted, "Here she is, the Goldman woman!" and at once a mob of screaming people rushed the bus, trying to get at Emma. Racing his engine, the quick-witted driver tore away, losing the mob.

At their hotel Emma and Ben were locked into their room on the top floor. "The Vigilantes are in an ugly mood," explained the worried hotel manager, Mr. Holmes. "They are determined to drive you both out of town." He said they must allow themselves to be locked in if they wished to stay in his hotel.

He was right. The Vigilantes *were* in an ugly mood. Toward evening the streets around the hotel filled up with a mass of cars and angry people. Horns blew, people whistled and screamed, sirens whined.

"The Vigilantes," said Ben, looking out the window.

Someone knocked at the door. It was Mr. Holmes, with two other men. "You are wanted downstairs," said Mr. Holmes.

They all went down together into a small room. Seven men stood waiting in a semicircle. Outside the horns and whistles were still blaring.

Presently the chief of police arrived. He asked Emma to step next door with him where the mayor was waiting to talk to her. As she and Ben got up to follow him, he turned to Ben and said, "You are not wanted, doctor. Better wait here." Then he walked quickly out of the room with Emma.

As soon as the door closed, the seven men pulled out guns and closed in on Ben.

"If you utter a sound or make a move we'll kill you," said one of them.

They grabbed him by the coat and each arm and led him outside. A car was waiting with the motor running. They threw him in and piled in beside him. The car drove slowly down the main street, the screaming mob after it, and then continued on out of town.

As soon as the city was behind them, the men in the car began to beat Ben. They took turns pulling his long hair and sticking their fingers into his ears and eyes. "We could tear your guts out," said one, "but we promised the chief of police not to kill you." He jabbed Ben hard in the small of the back.

At the county line the car pulled to a stop and everyone got out. The men formed a ring around Ben and tore off all his clothes. They kicked and beat him unconscious. With a lighted cigar one of the men burned the initials IWW into his buttocks. Another stuffed filth into his nose and ears. Still another poured a can of tar over his head and rubbed sagebrush, instead of feathers, onto his bruised, tarred body.

Then, ceremoniously, in his cloak of sage, Ben was

made to sing "The Star-Spangled Banner" and to kneel
to kiss the American flag.

What had made these Vigilantes so brutal? Surely
they did not honor the flag by raising it over such grotesque and obscene violence. They were victims of that
mass madness of perverted patriotism which Emma had
described the night Private William Buwalda had inno-
cently shaken her hand.

When Ben rose from that kiss, tears streaming
from his eyes and filth oozing from his nose, his tormen-
tors had him deliver a "patriotic" speech. After he had
spoken to their satisfaction, they made him "run the
gauntlet" through a double row of Vigilantes. Each man
delivered a blow or a kick to him as he passed by, as if
to leave a personal signature upon his body.

Now the ritual was over. The Vigilantes gave him
back his underwear and vest, his money and watch, and
his railroad ticket to Los Angeles. At last, turning him
toward the railroad tracks, they gave him a shove and
let him go.

Emma, meanwhile, returning from her talk with
the mayor, had found Ben missing. The mayor had offered her "protection" to get out of town. Where was
Ben's protection?

"What have you done with him?" she demanded of
the chief of police. "Where is Reitman?" she asked Mr.
Holmes. No one could give her an answer.

She paced her room anxiously, knowing there was not
one thing she could do. Was Ben alive or dead? At mid-

night she dozed off and dreamed she saw Ben, bound and gagged, groping for her with his beautiful narrow hands. But she, in her dream, was unable to reach or help him.

She woke with a start. Someone was banging on her door. Ben? She was sweating and her heart tripped. Quickly she opened the door.

There was one of the detectives, telling her that Ben had been put on a Los Angeles-bound train by the Vigilantes, and that she had better hurry there herself to receive him.

Emma leaped into her clothes and dashed to the station in a taxi. She could still catch the 2:45 A.M. train, the Owl, if she was lucky. As she reached the station in the dead of night she heard the sirens and horns of the Vigilantes. They were right behind her. She boarded the train and locked her compartment only seconds before the screaming mob appeared on the platform.

The next day in Los Angeles Emma received an anonymous phone call. The caller said Ben would be arriving on an afternoon train. Then he hadn't left San Diego after all! Emma thought. "You'd better bring a stretcher to the station," said the voice on the phone.

"Is he alive?" asked Emma frantically. "Is he still alive?" But no one answered her.

When the afternoon train steamed into Los Angeles, Ben was lying in a rear car, all huddled up. His cowboy hat was gone; his beautiful thick black curls were all sticky with tar. His face was deathly pale, and there was a look of terror in his eyes.

Emma stared at him in disbelief. What agony showed in his crumpled posture!

Finally he caught sight of Emma. He gazed at her silently for a long moment. Then softly he whimpered, "Oh take me away. Take me home."

The former King of the Hobos had sacrificed more for his subjects than they could ever have expected or imagined. The Queen of the Anarchists took him home.

14

The Woman Question

*And [Adam's] rib, which the Lord God had
taken from man, made he a woman. . . . And
unto the woman he said . . . thy desire shall be to
thy husband, and he shall rule over thee.*

—GENESIS

Ben Reitman was a strange man. His tastes, his quirks,
and his egotism never gave Emma any peace. He lied to
her about other women. He disappeared for days at a
time. He stole her money. He sulked about her friendship with Sasha, about money, about everything. But
Emma felt there was one thing Ben gave her that no
other man ever had. He loved her not only for her sex
and not only for her work but for both. No other man
had ever done so.

Sasha, Emma felt, had put the Cause ahead of everything and had loved her "with his head, not with his heart." Ed Brady had wanted "merely the woman" in her. Others had been attracted by her celebrity. But Ben, though he loved her with an intense passion, wanted to share in her work and devote his life to it. Women often did as much for the men they loved, but it was a rare thing for a man to do for a woman. Deep down most men considered women sex objects, and somehow inferior to men; women suffered from that opinion all their lives. Ben, Emma thought, was the rare exception.

Emma herself had had to pay for being female as far back as she could remember. Every morning at his prayers an orthodox Jewish man thanked his God that he was not born a slave or a woman. No wonder Emma's father had felt "cheated" to have first fathered a girl instead of a boy. No wonder that he had eagerly tried to marry his daughter off at the first opportunity. It was the acceptable way. A girl's life was not her own to settle, but her father's, and after that her husband's. A girl was part commodity to be traded and used.

Emma, however, had rebelled at the traditional way. She had always thought of herself as a person, not a thing. Female or not, she wanted to choose her life and her mate for herself. It had always seemed to her senseless and cruel that girls should be treated differently from boys. Boys were free to play, to talk, to work as they liked, but girls always had to be watched and protected. Boys had a right to be educated, while for girls education was a rare luxury. ("Girls do not have to learn much," Emma remembered her father saying;

only "how to prepare minced fish, cut noodles fine, and give the man plenty of children.")

As a child in Popelan Emma had seen another appalling inequality. When the young men and soldiers of the district made the local girls pregnant, it was the girls who were called names and driven from their homes or jobs and made to live in disgrace. Nothing happened to the young men. Emma had seen one miserable girl after another fired from her father's inn simply because she had become pregnant by some young man who was never blamed. Once she had felt so sorry for a pregnant serving girl that she had stolen coins from her mother's purse to give to her.

Like all girls, Emma was raised to believe that marriage would be the frosting on her life. But the married women Emma knew seemed more miserable than the single girls. Her mother, her aunts, the neighbor women—all of them were worn out by a lifetime of bickering and drudgery. All had to bow to the will of their husbands. With more work to do and more children to raise than they could ever manage, their domestic lives, Emma felt, were debased and sordid. And their domestic lives, it seemed, were the only lives they had.

Emma early realized that being born female was in some ways as bad as being born Jewish, or Russian, or even poor. As a Jew she might be forced to live in a ghetto; as a Russian she would have to submit to the decrees of the czar; as a member of the lowest economic class she might live forever in poverty. But as a girl, she was in danger of being given away to some man who would have absolute and permanent control over her entire life, even over her body. Not only was such power legal, it was supposed to be desirable! So completely was one half of the human race dominated by the other half that most women did not even protest. They simply accepted it as the way of the world.

In her teens in St. Petersburg Emma had learned about another kind of woman. The liberated Russian revolutionary women, like the young Vera Zasulich who had attacked the governor of St. Petersburg, followed their own desires, not those of their men. They lived alongside men, free and equal. If they sacrificed their lives it was for their own ideals, no one else's, and they did so as bravely as any man.

Though Emma had decided to try to live as they did, at first it had been hard for her. After fleeing to America she had rushed, lonely and discontented, straight into a disastrous marriage. Too late she realized that "binding people for life was wrong." What she had needed was love, not marriage—two very different things. Love, "the deepest element in all life," was natural and free; marriage was artificial and restricting. Free love and marriage were opposites. "If I ever love a man again," she had confided to Sasha after her divorce, "I will give myself to him without being bound by the rabbi or the law, and when that love dies I will leave without permission."

It was not because she took love lightly that she rejected marriage, but because she took it seriously. Love, with its free sexual expression, seemed to Emma "the most powerful moulder of human destiny." It could never be bought, or bound by marriage. "While it is true that some marriages are based on love," she wrote in an essay on marriage, "and in some cases love continues in married life, I maintain that it does so regardless of marriage, and not because of it."

A feminist is one who insists on the rights of women. Believing that women must have the same freedom in their lives as men, Emma had been something of a feminist most of her life. When she became an anarchist, her feminism grew even stronger. She began to see the connection between the institution of marriage and the other oppressive institutions of capitalism and State. Marriage was derived from the concept of private property, with the woman as the property. Marriage made woman into a domestic drudge, exploiting her as cheap labor. When a man married a woman he bought himself a domestic worker and a sex object, a breeder. In exchange, he promised the woman economic security. For a woman, marriage was like life insurance, but few women realized the price of the premiums. By accepting economic security, woman condemned herself to lifelong dependency, a high and degrading price.

Emma took great pains to express her views on love, sex, and marriage clearly and honestly. Still she was continually misunderstood, even by certain anarchists. There were the French anarchists at the Paris Anarchist Conference of 1900, for example. They had prevented her from reading a paper on "free love" and she had walked out of the conference because of it. Even the great Peter Kropotkin thought that Emma overemphasized the importance of sexual freedom for women. He considered woman's oppression mental, not sexual.

"When a woman is man's equal intellectually and shares in his social ideals, she will be as free as he," he told Emma.

To Emma's mind he was putting the problem backward. How could woman become man's equal intellectually when she was put down as his inferior and treated as a sexual commodity all her life? To think freely, a woman would first have to be free.

They argued and argued. Finally Emma said, "All right, dear comrade, when I have reached your age, the sex question may no longer be of importance to me. But it is *now*, and it is a tremendous factor to thousands, millions even, of young people."

Kropotkin stopped short and looked quizzically at his young friend. "Fancy," he said, "I didn't think of that. Perhaps you are right after all."

If certain anarchists were squeamish about Emma's discussions of sex and free love, the prudish public was scandalized. Though most of the attachments Emma formed with men were deep and lasting, she was commonly thought sex-mad. It was surprising. She did not make a cult of sex as some people did. And she looked nothing like the wild temptress the public feared. As a young woman she had indeed been both pretty and engaging. "A little bit of a girl, just five feet high including her boot heels, not showing her 120 pounds, with a saucy turned-up nose and very expressive blue-grey eyes," wrote a reporter of her when Emma was in her twenties. But by the time she took on "the woman question" in earnest, she was middle-aged, showing all of her spreading pounds, and as her novelist friend Frank Harris put it, "clearly not for ornament." She wore thick-lensed glasses that lent her eyes a fierce expression. America's leading advocate of free love resembled any-one's grandmother more than a stereotyped seductress. Her considerable glamour was glamour of spirit. "I would not pay for such foolishness as curled hair," she scornfully told a friend. Yet the public turned her into a symbol of sin and imagined her its own way.

Once Emma was lecturing in Reno, Nevada, America's easy divorce center. It was a place where, said Emma, "a certain class of women flock . . . to buy their freedom from one owner in order to sell themselves more profitably to another." Most of the women in Emma's hotel were awaiting their divorces. When they heard that Emma Goldman, "the champion of free love," was staying in the same hotel with them, they made the hotelkeeper get rid of her. It was as if her very presence could corrupt them.

To Emma such prudery—such puritanism—was pure hypocrisy. She knew from experience that "sex expression is as vital as food and air." Yet most Americans either pretended that there was no sex urge, or branded it as wicked. What was even more appalling, they condemned it for women and permitted it to men. America had a "double standard" of morality: one set of rules for women and an entirely different set for men. This double standard, which was one of the worst excesses of puritanism, victimized women. It was women who were disgraced by pregnancy, not the men who made them pregnant. It was women adulterers who could be deprived of their children, never male adulterers. Women who did not marry were expected to live without sex, while men were permitted sex whether or not they married. In every vice raid, it was the prostitutes who were arrested and sent to prison, never their male customers.

This last injustice seemed to Emma particularly outrageous. For wasn't it puritanism that made men want to buy what poverty forced women to sell? Just as it was prohibition of alcohol that made drunkenness more widespread (in New York City 15,000 legal bars were replaced by 32,000 illegal ones when drinking was outlawed), so prohibiting sexual freedom made prostitution thrive. In a frank and perceptive essay on prostitution, Emma wrote:

> Nowhere is woman treated according to the merit of her work, but rather as a sex. It is therefore almost inevitable that she should pay for her right to exist . . . with sex favors. Thus, it is merely a question of degree whether she sells herself to one man, in or out of marriage, or to many men. Whether our reformers admit it or not, the economic and social inferiority of women is responsible for prostitution.

What puritan, what moralistic reformer, could bear to hear such an attack on traditional feminine virtue, however true? The January 1910 issue of *Mother Earth,* in which the essay first appeared, was suppressed by the Post Office.

Emma's liberty-loving feminism offended not only the puritans and reformers. Many traditional feminists,

the army of women who campaigned for woman suffrage (the right to vote) also considered Emma the
enemy.

The suffragists, as these campaigners were called, believed that women would be equal with men as soon as
they won the right to vote. As an anarchist, Emma did
not believe that casting an occasional ballot was valuable to anyone. She certainly could not expect it to put
an end to the deep-rooted oppression of women. Getting the vote was a drop in the ocean; the suffragists
were wasting their energy. "Life, happiness, joy, freedom, independence—all that, and more, is [expected]
to spring from suffrage," Emma wrote. Such expectations were far too simple.

> Woman's development, her freedom, her indepen-
> dence, must come from and through herself. First by
> asserting herself as a personality, and not as a sex com-
> modity. Second, by refusing the right to anyone over
> her body; by refusing to bear children, unless she
> wants them; by refusing to be a servant to God, the
> State, society, the husband, the family, etc., by making
> her life simpler, but deeper and richer. That is, by
> trying to learn the meaning and substance of life in all
> its complexities, by freeing herself from the fear of
> public opinion and public condemnation. Only that,
> and not the ballot, will set woman free.

As she delivered her lectures glorifying freedom and be-
littling the value of the vote, the women in the audience would frequently hoot and shout, "You are a man's
woman!" and "You are an enemy of woman's freedom!"

The suffrage movement was a thoroughly middle-class movement. It was not revolutionary, and Emma would not support it. Demanding the vote in the name of virtue, family, and home, most suffragists hoped to eliminate the double standard by bringing men under the same rigid rules as women. Emma wanted instead to eliminate those rules for everyone, men and women alike.

If Emma's views on the "woman question" were somewhat different from the views of other feminists, they were staggeringly different from the views of conservative Americans. "The prime duty of the average woman is to be a good wife and mother," said President Theodore Roosevelt. Former President Grover Cleveland went even further. In the May 1905 *Ladies' Home Journal* he said that every activity of a woman outside the home was dangerous to society. The spread of women's clubs was alarming; suffragism was a disease. The "womanly traits that distinguish us above other nations, and the strength and beauty of our domestic life, are put in peril," he warned, by every woman who wants to join a club or cast a vote.

> What a blessed thing it would be if every mother, and every woman, whether mother, wife, spinster, or maid, who . . . desires for woman a greater share in the direction of public affairs, could realize the everlasting truth that "the hand that rocks the cradle is the hand that rules the world."

All nonsense, thought Emma, dangerous nonsense. But to people who held such opinions, Emma's views were dangerous. Emma's dazzling disregard of all the conventions—her public smoking, drinking, speaking, organizing, and agitating—were shocking. But her outspoken views on love, sex, and marriage were worse than shocking. When, in 1915, she actually began to give public lectures on how to practice birth control, she finally went too far. That kind of talk was against the law. Surely she would be locked away again.

Emma's interest in birth control went back to her earliest nursing days. As a midwife in the slums of New York she had watched with horror as one wretched woman after another gave birth to a child she didn't want. Emma herself had been told years before that because of an early illness she would have to have an operation if she wanted to bear children. She had decided not to have it. Though she loved children, she knew there would be no room in her life for a child of her own. Every woman, she felt, had a right to make the same choice. If a woman wanted children, she ought to be able to have as many as she wanted without marrying. If she chose not to have a child, she ought to be able to have love and sex anyway. Every woman should have absolute control over her own body and her own motherhood. Many so-called "emancipated" women, who refused to marry and supported themselves, had given up men altogether. Though they escaped bondage to a husband, they were often lonely and in some ways no freer than married women. For them and for married women alike, part of the problem was their own attitudes about sex. But another part could be solved by birth control.

As soon as she learned about birth-control methods at the Neo-Malthusian Conference of 1900, Emma began lecturing on the subject. It was not until 1915, however, that she courted arrest by telling how to use birth-control devices. By 1915 the birth-control movement, led by Margaret Sanger and others, had aroused considerable liberal support. The time seemed ripe for a showdown with the sanctimonious establishment. The arrest of Margaret Sanger's husband for giving someone one of Margaret's pamphlets served as a signal to Emma. She felt she too must risk arrest—or else stop lecturing on the subject. There had been enough talk; it was time to act.

On March 28, 1915, in New York City's popular liberal discussion forum, the Sunrise Club, Emma stood up and frankly explained to a mixed audience of 600 people how to practice birth control. It was the first time the subject had been publicly discussed anywhere in America. With an arrest expected, it was fitting that Emma should be the speaker. Whenever the authorities were hacking at a limb, Emma was likely to be out on it. Her supporters came to the hall with bail money for her. She came, as usual, with a book to read in jail.

The lecture went well. Emma spoke as frankly as she would have on any medical subject. Afterward she was complimented for her "clear and natural" presentation. Of the many respectable doctors, lawyers, artists, businessmen, and their wives who made up the audience, no one fainted and only a few snickered.

To everyone's surprise, Emma was not arrested. She wondered why the police ignored this deliberate violation of the law when they had so often arrested her for breaking no law at all. She would simply give the lecture again. And again. She would spread the word on birth control until she was stopped by force. Packing up the birth-control devices, she set off with Ben on another grand tour.

Back again in New York early in 1916, she was finally arrested. The following week Ben was arrested too.

Emma's and Ben's arrests produced exactly the result they hoped for. Reformers were outraged. There were protests all around the country. People were beginning to feel that they had a right to obtain birth-control information. At a huge protest meeting in New York's Carnegie Hall, the radical wife of a wealthy socialite personally passed out copies of the same information for which Emma had been arrested. In San Francisco forty of the city's leading women declared in writing that they were ready to go to jail for passing out birth-control leaflets, and promptly did so.

On April 20 Emma's case went to trial. Emma defended herself. Three staid judges presided over an overflowing courtroom. Emma, as always, was expected to put on the best show in town.

After some witty exchanges with the prosecutor, Emma turned her trial into an eloquent defense of birth control. Her closing speech to the court lasted for one rapturous hour. "If it is a crime," she concluded with passion, "to work for healthy motherhood and happy child-life, I am proud to be considered a criminal!"

"Guilty," came the judges' verdict, and Emma was

sentenced either to pay a fine of $100 or to serve fifteen days in jail. As paying fines was a privilege of the rich, Emma proudly chose jail. The entire courtroom rose and cheered her.

The following week Ben was tried, found guilty, and sentenced to sixty days.

As soon as their sentences were up, Emma and Ben went right back into the battle. Again and again they were arrested; again and again they returned to the fight. Mostly, they were acquitted, or the charges against them were dropped. But not always. Once Ben was arrested in Cleveland for calling for volunteers to distribute birth-control pamphlets after one of Emma's lectures. A hundred cheering people followed him to jail, each one waving the forbidden pamphlet. But Ben alone was jailed. He was sentenced to six months and fined $1,000.

With all the arrests and trials and protests, Emma and Ben succeeded in helping to spread birth-control information all over the country. It easily became a burning issue. Even some of the judges were won over. "I believe we are living in an age of ignorance," said one judge, "which at some future time will be looked upon aghast as we now look upon the dark ages." Such success made Emma say "it was certainly worth going to jail."

But Emma never forgot that society's injustice to women went much deeper than the matters of birth control or the vote or discriminatory laws. It went all the way, as reformers never did, "to the bottom of things." Girls, she noted, are told from infancy "that marriage is the ultimate goal." They are raised to serve others, not themselves. Thousands of women, she observed, have "sacrificed their own talents and ambitions for the sake of the man. But few men have done so for women," with Ben, of course, the exception.

Years later, when she was fifty-two, Emma fell in love with a man much younger than she. In a touching letter to him she lamented that "traditions of centuries have created the cruel injustice which grants to the man the right to ask and receive love from one much younger than himself and does not grant the same right to the woman." These "traditions of centuries" could not be wiped out by surface reforms, however urgent or sweeping or numerous. They had to be changed at the root, by revolution. Suffragists, liberalizers of the laws, and other reformers were interested in freeing women only from the "external tyrants," as Emma called them. But women needed to free themselves from the internal tyrants as well: from "ethical and social conventions," "public opinion," or "what-will-mother-say." With shrewd insight Emma predicted that "until woman has learned to defy them all . . . she cannot call herself emancipated."

Time was to prove all Emma's predictions correct. In 1920 a constitutional amendment granted American women the vote, and immediately afterward the feminist movement fell apart. It was not revived till the late 1960's. With the vote, women gained little equality and even less freedom. Discriminatory laws remained on the statute books. The double standard persisted. Job and wage discrimination continued. Domestic and sexual exploitation of women went on as they always had. And Emma, who predicted it all, was by that time banished from America, soon to be forgotten.

15

Conspiracy for Peace

Every conspiracy is by its very nature secret; a case can hardly be supposed where men concert together for crime and advertise their purpose to the world.
—SUPREME COURT JUSTICE JOHN M. HARLAN, 1957

The slaughter now known as World War I had erupted in Europe in 1914. In 1916 the United States, though officially neutral, was still trying to decide whether or not to enter the war.

Emotions ran high on both sides. Hundreds of thousands of people clamored for the government to arm itself and prepare for war. "Preparedness" was the slogan of the day. At the same time, many other Americans just as loudly counseled peace. Among the earliest and most active pacifists was Emma. All her active life she had denounced every war she had lived through. To her, as to most anarchists, war was nothing but a tool of government and capitalism. It was simply the bloodiest of the many ways governments use to increase their own power at the expense of the people. A people's war, a revolution, was the only exception.

Since her release from jail, Emma had been devoting more and more effort to denouncing the war and the American military buildup. It seemed to her quite the most important issue. She even set aside the birth-control fight for it. "Preparedness," she thought, would only insure that the United States would join in the international slaughter.

On July 22, 1916, Emma was enjoying a leisurely lunch with Sasha and his young companion Eleanor Fitzgerald ("Fitzi") in their San Francisco apartment. With Fitzi to help him, Sasha had moved to San Francisco earlier in the year to edit a new anarchist-labor weekly called *Blast*. Now Emma, in town on a lecture tour, was visiting him. It was a tense day. In the streets below 100,000 people had gathered to watch the Preparedness Parade. The parade, sponsored by the San Francisco Law and Order Committee, seemed to Emma but one more sign that the "war madness" was overtaking the country.

Sasha was in the middle of an amusing story when the telephone rang. He excused himself and went to answer it. When he returned to the table, the expression on his face told Emma something was wrong.

"A bomb exploded in the Preparedness Parade," he said grimly. "There are killed and wounded."

"I hope they aren't going to hold the anarchists responsible for it," Emma cried.

"How could they?" asked Fitzi.

"How could they not?" answered Sasha. "They always have."

They did; that very day. Ten people had been killed and forty more wounded by the explosion. The newspapers reporting the tragedy carried front-page headlines about "Anarchist Bombs."

Emma had been scheduled to deliver a lecture two nights before the parade on "Preparedness—the Road to Universal Slaughter." It was only by a stroke of luck that she happened to postpone the lecture. If she hadn't, everyone would certainly have blamed her for the tragedy.

The San Francisco district attorney thought the case a splendid opportunity to advance his political career. First he tried to connect Emma with the bombing but failed for lack of evidence. Next he tried to pin it on five San Francisco labor agitators. This time he managed to have the five radicals indicted for murder, though there was as little evidence against them as there had been against Emma. Actually, no one was ever to discover who did throw the bomb. But the district attorney felt that someone had to be prosecuted.

Though only one of the accused was an anarchist, all five were friends of Sasha. Convinced of their innocence, Sasha rushed to their defense. In the beginning, only he and Emma defended the accused—Sasha in the pages of *Blast,* Emma from the lecture platform. Hoping to implicate Sasha, the police raided the office of

Blast and ransacked the files. But for the time being Sasha escaped arrest.

Warren Billings was the first of the five to be tried and found guilty. In October, 1916, he was sentenced to life imprisonment. Thomas Mooney was tried next and found guilty. The following February he was sentenced to hang.

The trials had been scandalously rigged by the district attorney, who bribed the witnesses and tampered with the juries. Eventually the witnesses would confess and the entire frame-up would be exposed. But until that happened, Sasha had an enormous job to do if Mooney's life was to be saved.

Then suddenly, desperate to save Mooney, Emma and Sasha hit on a brilliant plan. It depended on events occurring halfway around the world. During the same month that Mooney had been sentenced to die, a political revolution had shaken Russia. The February Revolution of 1917 had replaced the czar's terrorist government with a temporary revolutionary government. Thousands of Russians exiled in America had begun returning to their homeland. Emma and Sasha had wanted to join them, but they had felt a duty to stay in America to save Mooney and denounce the rapidly approaching war. Instead of returning, they asked some of their friends who were going back to organize a Russian protest for Mooney.

On April 22, 1917, in the streets of St. Petersburg, thousands of Russian workers gathered under the windows of the United States Embassy chanting, "Mooney, Mooney."

"Who or what is Mooney?" asked the ambassador, and wired Washington to see about it. He would learn who Mooney was soon enough.

Emma's and Sasha's plan was more successful than even they had imagined. It was so successful that the tactic would be copied many times over in years to come. Newspapers all over Europe publicized the story of Mooney. There were similar demonstrations in Rome, Paris, London. The United States was accused of keeping the radical Mooney a "political prisoner"— someone imprisoned for his political opinions. The matter became an international scandal.

At home, the nation suddenly learned about the San Francisco frame-up. People rushed to aid Sasha's Mooney-Billings Defense Committee, contributing $10,000 in one month. Leaving nothing to chance, Sasha induced an influential friend to go to Washington and see to it that the Mooney case was kept under President Woodrow Wilson's nose.

Six days before Mooney was to hang, President Wilson wrote a letter to the governor of California. "In view of certain international aspects which the case has assumed," he wrote, he would appreciate it if the governor would kindly postpone Mooney's execution. Then the president appointed a committee of dignitaries to investigate the entire affair.

In San Francisco the district attorney was furious. Knowing that Emma and Sasha were behind the investigation, he vowed to get Sasha. "I should have murdered Berkman!" said an assistant district attorney to a reporter.

In April President Wilson, who had run for office as a peace candidate, had asked Congress to declare war on Germany "to make the world safe for democracy." It would be "the war to end war," he proclaimed, and many pacifists switched their support to the war effort. Not Emma. With the country at war, her antiwar campaign seemed to her all the more urgent. A Draft Bill was before Congress that would require that all young men between twenty-one and thirty register for conscription into the army. As fast as she could, Emma organized a No-Conscription League and stepped up her campaign.

President Wilson signed the Draft Bill into law, and June 4 was set as Registration Day. That day, said Emma, "American democracy would be carried to its grave."

Hundreds of young men began telephoning the No-Conscription League and streaming into its offices for help and advice. Hundreds more sought help in other branches of the League that opened in other cities. Without actually advising anyone not to register, Emma and Sasha, in print and in person, did everything they could to denounce the war and the draft. The war-bent nation was whipped to a frenzy against the pacifists. Newspapers raged at their defiance of the new law and denounced them all as traitors. Each antidraft rally the pacifists held became more tense and dangerous than the last.

At a peace rally in New York's Madison Square Garden, several young pacifists were arrested and charged with conspiracy. Their crime was handing out announcements of Emma's Registration Day rally. One pacifist was sentenced to two years in prison.

At the next rally Emma sensed trouble as soon as she arrived. Outside the hall stood police with machine guns. Inside, many soldiers were in the audience. Soon after the speeches began, screaming soldiers in the balconies started unscrewing light bulbs from the fixtures and throwing them at the stage. Asked to stop them, the police in the hall did nothing. Finally a soldier shouted, "Let's charge the platform!" Some of the audience tried to grab him. The police readied their clubs. Everyone tensed for a fight.

Suddenly it struck Emma that the police and the hecklers might be in league. Perhaps they were promoting a riot in order to arrest the pacifists. She leaped to the platform and cried, "Friends, friends—wait, wait!" Then, as she had done several times before, she persuaded the audience to file out calmly. "If we lose our heads there will be bloodshed, and it will be our blood they will shed!" she said, and declared the meeting closed.

Emma had succeeded that night in averting a riot, but the next day newspapers reported a riot anyway. After that hardly a hall in New York could be rented for antidraft meetings.

On June 14 Emma and her friends were able to hold one last meeting before the end. It was a meeting they would always regret. As soon as it was over, the police stopped all draft-age men on the way out and demanded to see their draft registration. Those without their papers were arrested.

The next day a horde of detectives burst into the offices of *Mother Earth* and *Blast,* recently moved from California to New York.

"Emma Goldman," said the federal marshal, "you're under arrest. And so is Berkman."

Emma looked around. The detectives had already started searching her files. "Where is your warrant?" she asked.

There was no warrant, neither to arrest nor to search. Instead of a warrant the marshal produced a copy of the June issue of *Mother Earth*. It was the issue containing Emma's No-Conscription Manifesto, which the Post Office had tried to suppress. The cover showed a coffin draped in black, with the words: IN MEMORIAM— AMERICAN DEMOCRACY.

"No warrant necessary," said the marshal. *Mother Earth,* he said, was incriminating enough to put her in jail for years.

Emma and Sasha were charged with conspiracy to obstruct the draft. Their bail was set preposterously high —$25,000 each. The government officials had waited a long time to get the two "most dangerous anarchists in America." Now that they had them, they were not eager to let them go.

On June 27, 1917, less than two weeks after their arrest, Emma and Sasha went on trial for conspiracy. It was Emma's forty-eighth birthday.

They acted as their own attorneys. They had each stood trial before, and they had defended themselves before. But this was the first time they were being tried together. Though they did not yet know it, their American careers were drawing to an end. It was fitting that the comrades should end them, as they had begun them, together.

It was hot and sticky as the trial finally got under way. On the street just below the packed courtroom an army recruiting station had been set up. From time to time strains of "The Star-Spangled Banner," played by a military band, floated up through the windows. Whenever the music began, everyone in the courtroom was ordered to stand up. Those who didn't were removed from the courtroom by a guard. The guards could hardly remove the defendants, however, and Emma and Sasha stubbornly remained seated.

The two defendants were charged not with *interfering with the draft,* but with *"conspiracy" to interfere with the draft.* The "conspiracy" charge was an old government trick to make conviction relatively easy. A handy weapon against political "criminals," the conspiracy charge usually allowed for heavier penalties than the "crime" it was attached to. To prove "conspiracy," the prosecution had only to establish the defendants' *intention* to do something illegal. Whether or not they actually *did* anything to interfere with the draft did not matter. It was as though *plotting* to commit a robbery were worse than actually committing one.

Sasha handled the conspiracy question deftly and with wit. He declared that since he and his codefendant had been openly opposing militarism for twenty-eight years, their "conspiracy" was well known to a hundred million people. That could hardly, he said, be called "conspiracy" at all.

The prosecution tried to prove many things for which Emma and Sasha were not even on trial. They attacked the defendants' characters. They tried to show that the defendants advocated violence. They suggested that the defendants were being paid by the Germans. But they could not prove that the defendants had advised young men not to register for the draft; the defendants hadn't done so. Finally, they used Emma's and Sasha's published statements to try to prove "conspiracy."

Emma, in turn, argued her case with calm and logic. She even impressed the judge. She called a number of famous and respected American radicals to testify for the defense: John Reed, Lincoln Steffens, Bolton Hall all stepped forward to speak for her.

When at last all the evidence had been presented and all the witnesses had testified, Emma and Sasha delivered their closing speeches. It was the moment they had been waiting for. At last, together, they could speak out to a captive America. Sasha spoke for two hours, Emma for one, holding the court rapt the entire time. They talked movingly of anarchism and democracy, liberty and law. When they were finished, the judge turned to address the jury. "In the conduct of this case the defendants have shown remarkable ability. An ability which might have been utilized for the great benefit of this country, had they seen fit to employ themselves in behalf of it rather than against it." He advised the jury not to consider "whether the defendants are right or wrong," but only whether or not they were guilty. Then he sent them to reach a verdict.

Thirty-nine minutes later the jury returned to the courtroom. The defendants, they said, were guilty.

Immediately the judge imposed the maximum sentence, two years in prison and a $10,000 fine for each. He recommended that when their sentences were up, they be deported. "For such people as would nullify our laws," he said, "we have no place in our country."

Emma and Sasha were in prison only a short time when the Supreme Court agreed to review their case. They were ordered back to a New York jail, where new bail was set for them. Arriving in New York, they learned that Sasha had finally been indicted for murder in San Francisco, in connection with the Mooney case. California authorities had asked New York to turn Sasha over to them.

Emma was bailed out at once; Sasha was not. With a murder charge against him, his friends felt he would be safer in jail than free. The California authorities might kidnap him off the street if he were free, but they would have to go through formal extradition proceedings to snatch him from jail in New York. No one doubted that if he were transferred to California he would be framed and convicted as Tom Mooney had been.

Once free, Emma joined Sasha's friend Fitzi in fighting against Sasha's extradition. They formed a Defense Committee to approach the New York governor, and they sent a secret message to their friends in Russia about the charge against Sasha. "Uncle sick of the same disease as Tom. Tell friends," read the coded cable. Immediately mass demonstrations took place in St. Petersburg and Kronstadt, with Berkman's name added to those of Mooney and Billings.

The Defense Committee organized a mass rally for Sasha at a large New York theater for September 11, 1917. Emma was to be the chief speaker. Just before the audience was due to arrive, a federal marshal informed Emma that he would lock the audience out of the theater unless she promised not to speak.

It was the old story again. Ordinarily Emma refused on principle to comply with a policeman's threats, but this time she knew it was crucial that the rally take place. Sasha's life might depend on it. Reluctantly she gave the marshal her promise not to speak, and she took a seat in the audience.

The last speaker was on stage. Angrily he explained why Emma had not appeared. "The marshal has gagged Emma, too stupid to realize that her voice will now carry far beyond the walls of this theater!"

At that very moment, out onto the stage marched Emma. Keeping her promise to the marshal, she faced the audience without a word. But in her mouth she had stuffed a large white handkerchief.

It brought down the house. The crowd laughed and stamped their feet and screamed their pleasure. Even in silence, Emma simply could not be shut up.

In St. Petersburg, meanwhile, anarchist sailors of nearby Kronstadt approached the United States ambassador. They threatened to hold him as a hostage until Mooney, Billings, and Berkman were released. Promising on the spot to work for the release of all "political prisoners," the ambassador immediately cabled Washington and then went into hiding.

After a series of letters, President Wilson prevailed on the governor of California to commute Mooney's death sentence once and for all. And the murder charge against Sasha was abandoned.

Free on bail, Sasha returned to fight for Mooney's freedom. Emma set off to publicize the "miracle" of the Russian Revolution. What had started in Russia in February as a political revolution had turned in November into an economic and social revolution as well. Although the revolutionary Bolshevik Party had formed a powerful government, Emma supported it. She believed it was committed to political freedom and economic equality. She believed that the revolution anarchists had longed for and the revolution of the Bolsheviks in Russia were one and the same.

While they campaigned, the Supreme Court decided Emma's and Sasha's case. The Draft Law, the court held, was fully legal; Emma's and Sasha's opposition to it was not. Even though the pair may not actually have interfered with the draft, they were still guilty of conspiracy. "A conspiracy to commit an offense, when followed by overt acts, is punishable as a crime, whether the illegal end is accomplished or not," wrote the chief justice. Decades would pass before the court would question that opinion.

Emma and Sasha published a last "farewell" to their friends. They said, "Be of good cheer, good friends and comrades. We are going to prison with light hearts. To us it is more satisfactory to stay behind bars than to remain MUZZLED in freedom."

On February 5, 1918, in the middle of the war, Emma and Sasha turned themselves in at the Federal Building in New York City. From there they were taken by train to prison—Sasha to Atlanta, Georgia, Emma to Jefferson City, Missouri. It was, Emma wrote a friend, "with the exalted sense of having remained absolutely true to my ideal" that she would live out her final American years in prison.

16

Red Scare

The Mayflower *brought the first of the builders to this country; the* Buford *has taken away the first destroyers.*
—EDITORIAL IN THE "SATURDAY EVENING POST,"
1920

When the United States entered the war with Germany, the country went mad with patriotism. America, Emma observed from her prison cell, seemed to be turning into a vast lunatic asylum, with the madmen on the out-side running things. Abroad, American soldiers were killing German soldiers. At home, superpatriots were hunting for spies behind every curtain and denouncing everything faintly German.

Hundreds of innocent German aliens were impris-oned without trials in the immigration camp on Ellis Island. In some states the German language was struck from school curricula. People with German-sounding names were attacked and even lynched.

"Patriotic" societies—from the government-sponsored American Protective League to the southern Ku Klux Klan—snowballed overnight into enormous clubs. They were suspicious of anyone who wasn't "100 percent American." Anyone who opposed the war was considered a traitor. The jails were filled with pacifists. Patriotic mobs whipped, tarred, and feathered people whose only offense was failure to support the Red Cross or to buy Liberty Bonds. A leader of the anarchistic IWW union, which had opposed the war, was dragged from his bed in the middle of the night and murdered.

Bad as the wartime hysteria was, the Red Scare that soon followed it was worse.

In March 1918 the United States lost an ally in the war against Germany. The new Bolshevik government of Russia, eager to get out of the "capitalist war," signed a separate peace treaty with Germany. This looked like a betrayal to many frantic Americans. They began hating Russians as well as Germans, and radical Russian sympathizers as well as German sympathizers.

In 1918 the war ended. The German enemy was vanquished. Now, still charged with the wartime hysteria, superpatriots turned their attention from the German enemy to the "enemy within": radicals. The German spy hunt became a radical witch hunt. Even the Congressional committee investigating Germans switched to investigating Reds, as radicals were called.

During the war all strikes had been outlawed for the sake of the war effort. With the war over, strikes became legal again, and many strikes were called all around the country. It was hardly surprising that unions should make use of their best weapon now that it was legal. But many newspapers proclaimed that the strikes were all part of some grand "communist plot." A great fear came over the land. Was there a vast Red conspiracy to take over the United States government as the Bolsheviks had taken over the government of Russia? A wave of bombings and riots convinced many people that there was. Fear deepened and spread like a disease.

May 1, May Day, had long been celebrated by workers around the world as world labor day. In the United States, on the day before May Day, 1919, three dozen small brown packages were mailed from New York to various public men. Packages were addressed to, among others, the millionaires John D. Rockefeller and J. P. Morgan; several United States senators and federal judges; two state governors; the district attorney in the Mooney case; and the attorney general of the United States, A. Mitchell Palmer.

One of the packages was delivered to Senator Hardwick of Georgia. His maid took it into the kitchen to open. As she opened it, an explosion shook the house. In the explosion the maid lost both her hands and the senator's wife was badly injured.

The package, like all the others, had contained a bomb. Who had sent it and why, no one ever found out. Fortunately most of the other thirty-five bombs never reached their intended victims. Those that did failed to go off. But across the country people began to panic. Anarchist bombs! they thought; Bolshevik plots! With no one person to blame, newspapers raged against all radicals.

The next day was May Day. Workers celebrated in every large city, marching in grand parades behind their traditional red banners. But in city after city enraged citizens disrupted the parades and police began attacking the marchers. In Boston, Cleveland, and New York the attacks grew into full-blown riots. Hundreds of paraders were beaten up and arrested. Their red flags were destroyed. Although in every case it was the antiradicals who started the riots, only radicals were arrested.

Newspapers announced that the Red revolution had begun in America. They demanded new laws to "curb Bolshevism." The spreading fear mounted to hysteria.

The next month, the hysteria finally turned to terror. One evening in early June, just as they were getting ready for bed, Attorney General Palmer and his wife were shocked by a mighty explosion. The front of their Washington house collapsed. Windows were shattered in houses for blocks around. Palmer and his family were so stunned that they could not even call the police. Their neighbor, the young Secretary of the Navy Franklin Delano Roosevelt, had to make the call for them. Eight other bombings occurred that night. Fear hung over Washington.

Now Congress rushed to act. Appropriating half a million dollars for Red hunting, they demanded that radicals be caught. With the money, Attorney General Palmer set up a special Antiradical Division of the Department of Justice's detective force. Later it would become the Federal Bureau of Investigation, the FBI.

Run by J. Edgar Hoover, who eventually became the chief of the FBI, the Antiradical Division collected all the information on radicals it could.

It was thought at the time that 90 percent of all radicals were aliens. Under the 1918 Alien Exclusion Act, any alien could be deported for merely believing in anarchism or not believing in government. Only the rights of citizens, not those of aliens, were protected by the Constitution. Aliens, lacking rights, were easy to get rid of. They did not even have the right to a trial. An alien could be deported on the basis of any scrap of evidence, no matter how trivial. No proof of lawbreaking was necessary. Suspicion was really enough.

In Washington, J. Edgar Hoover busily indexed the names of first "60,000 Reds," then 200,000, while Palmer laid his plans to catch and deport them. Many of the names on the list came from the confiscated private files of *Mother Earth* and *Blast*. Many others were the names of people not radical at all. According to the historian of the Red Scare, Robert K. Murray,

> by late 1919 a radical was anyone suspected of being pro-German, a Russian or other foreigner, a person who sent bombs through the mails, a believer in free love, a member of the IWW, a Socialist, a Bolshevist, an anarchist, a member of a labor union, . . . or anyone who did not particularly agree with you.

Tops on Palmer's list of undesirables were "the Red Queen" and "the Red King," Emma Goldman and Alexander Berkman.

While Palmer and Hoover plotted in Washington, a

thousand miles to the west, in a dank cell in the Missouri State Prison, Emma Goldman celebrated her fiftieth birthday. It was a fitting place, she observed, for a rebel's birthday party. In fifty years her ideals had proved stronger than the steel of all the bars she had ever been locked behind; each jailing only strengthened them. "It would be well," she once wrote to a friend from prison, "if every rebel were sent to prison for a time; it would fan his smouldering flame of hate of the things that make prisons possible." A half-century old and locked away, she was still as tenaciously idealistic as ever. Birthday gifts streamed into her cell from all over the country. They celebrated her courage and endurance more than her age. To many radicals in those days of terror, Emma Goldman's life was more than a symbol. It was an inspiration.

Even her conservative mother aging in Rochester took inspiration from Emma. The story goes that once at a club meeting the eighty-one-year-old Taube Goldman spoke a little too long. The chairman asked if she wouldn't please give someone else a turn to speak. Defiantly Mrs. Goldman refused, pointing out, "The whole United States government could not stop my daughter Emma Goldman from speaking, and a fine chance you have to make her mother shut up!"

Like many other radicals who spent the war years behind bars, Emma pushed for prison reforms. In her eyes the prisoners were not criminals, but simply the "butt of all the horrors," driven to crime by circumstances. By day she did everything she could for them. At night she turned to her own concerns.

Alone in her cell she read with alarm of the new American heresy hunt. Breathlessly she read reports of the New Russia. Each night she would transport herself from Missouri to Russia, where in her imagination she helped build the revolution.

Attorney General Palmer, meanwhile, was preparing to have her transported to Russia not in imagination but in reality. With her prison sentence almost up, he and J. Edgar Hoover were compiling a fat file of evidence against her. They had documents to show that she was not a citizen (because her former husband, Kershner, was not) and documents to show she was a dangerous radical. With them, they would have her deported. Richard Drinnon, in his biography of Emma, *Rebel in Paradise,* has carefully documented how the government worked systematically for years to get rid of her. Not only did the government use all the resources of a rich and powerful State to silence her, but it doctored documents, manufactured evidence, and coerced witnesses. There was very little that one person could do against such power—even a person as fearless and resourceful as Emma. In the end, she was vanquished by the very enemy she had spent her life denouncing: the all-powerful national State.

In September 1919 Emma was released from prison. Three days later Sasha was released. From then on everything happened quickly.

Within a month Emma was summoned to the immigration camp on Ellis Island for a deportation hearing. J. Edgar Hoover himself presented the case against her. He produced the record of her 1893 trial for inciting to riot, though she had already served her prison term for that offense. He produced old articles from *Mother Earth* to show Emma's belief in violence, though she herself had not written them and they had not been suppressed when they were published. He submitted a transcript of Czolgosz's 1901 confession, doctored to make it seem that Emma had been responsible for McKinley's assassination. None of these documents could have been used against her if she had been a citizen with Constitutional protections. But as an alien, she could be deported on the strength of any one of them. Only a "scintilla" of evidence against her was required.

Proud and defiant, Emma would have nothing to do with the hearing. It was a mockery of a just trial. When Hoover asked her questions, she sat, arms folded, firm and silent. She would answer no questions. Instead she handed Hoover a written statement. "I protest against these proceedings," it began, "as utterly tyrannical and . . . opposed to the fundamental guarantees of a true democracy. Every human being is entitled to hold any opinion that appeals to her or him without making herself or himself liable to persecution."

Sasha's deportation hearing had been held in prison just before his release. He had been kept in solitary confinement for an incredible, crippling seven and a half months, up until the day of his discharge. Broken physically, he nevertheless defied his questioners. He too refused to participate in his hearing. "Thought is, or should be, free. My social views and political opinions are my personal concern. I owe no one responsibility for them," his written statement said.

To prove it, as soon as he was released, he joined Emma in a public defense of the Russian Revolution. It was as though they had never stopped agitating, and as though they had nothing at stake. Until their cases were decided, whatever time they had left they would use as they always had.

Certain congressmen were appalled that the two most notorious anarchists in America were out on the street agitating. Why, wondered a senator, had they not already been deported? Why, demanded the newspapers, were there still thousands of alien radicals loose in the land? If there were certain legal barriers against prosecuting radical citizens, there were none to deporting radical aliens. The Department of Justice, Congress said, must move against them. Fast.

On November 7, 1919, Attorney General Palmer decided to act. In a dozen cities across the country federal agents carried out the first "Palmer raid." Many more would follow. With it, the worst phase of the Red Scare began.

Agents stormed into the offices of Russian workers' organizations, arresting 450 suspected Reds. Aliens were shipped to the immigration camp on Ellis Island in New York to await hearings and deportation. Citizens were turned over to local police. Palmer's first raid was the signal to superpatriots everywhere that they too might act. The next day a rash of local raids began. In New York City alone 500 more radicals were arrested by the police.

Mobs, particularly in the west, attacked radicals in union halls, on the streets, at their meeting places. In

West Virginia 118 strikers were attacked by a mob and forced to kiss the flag. The worst mob violence occurred in Centralia, Washington. When a group of American Legionnaires stormed the headquarters of the local IWW, armed Wobblies defended the hall. Three men were killed. Only Wobblies were arrested, though they hadn't started the battle. Late that night there was a mysterious power failure in Centralia. When the lights went on again, one Wobbly was missing from jail. He had been kidnapped, tortured, mutilated, and finally murdered by a gang of Vigilantes. Later his grotesque corpse was returned to the jail as an example to the other prisoners.

On it went, for two terrible months and more. Those months of mass hysteria came to be known as "Palmer's Reign of Terror." More than 3,000 men and women were arrested in the last months of 1919. Thousands more would be taken in 1920. Many of those arrested had no idea of what they were accused. Many other people, though not arrested, were persecuted by mobs. Describing the people caught in the raids, Palmer himself fanned the terror. He wrote: "Out of the sly and crafty eyes of many of them leap cupidity, cruelty, insanity, and crime; from their lopsided faces, sloping brows, and misshapen features may be recognized the unmistakable criminal type." But the truth was that few of the prisoners had ever committed any crime at all.

At the height of the terror Emma and Sasha set off on a tour to denounce the Palmer raids. Though her case might be jeopardized, Emma felt she must raise her voice "against the shame of my adopted land." On the tour, great crowds turned out to hear the anarchists speak. People had come to count on them for courage, for daring to say what others only thought.

They were lecturing in Chicago when the news came that their cases had been settled. A federal judge had ruled that Emma was not, and had never been, a United States citizen. Both she and Sasha were ordered deported as alien anarchists.

Emma had one last chance to stay the order. She could appeal the question of her citizenship to the Supreme Court. In Sasha's case, however, there was no appeal, for he had never claimed United States citizenship.

As always, Sasha urged Emma to put the revolution ahead of him. She must, he said, stay in America to appeal her case and establish her rights.

But Emma couldn't do it. Her life was too intimately tied to Sasha's for her to part from him now. They had been comrades for thirty years. She decided that wherever they went they must go together.

"It's no use, old scout," she said to Sasha firmly. "You can't get rid of me so easily. I have made my decision. I am going with you."

Half gratefully, Sasha gripped her hand. He said nothing more. He knew they would remain together now, no matter what might happen.

They took a train to New York, and from the station they went directly to Ellis Island to surrender. Their friends went with them, followed by reporters.

"This is the end, Emma Goldman, isn't it?" a reporter asked her.

"It may be only the beginning," Emma said.

Ellis Island was known as the Island of Tears. Though not officially a prison, people were held there for months and even years without trials. Families were separated and people with no ties outside the United States were deported.

The commissioner of immigration at Ellis Island at the time of the Red Scare was a reformer named Frederick Howe. Howe had tried to improve conditions on the island. But his hard work was ruined during the Red Scare as the place turned from an Island of Tears to an Island of Terror. The deportation hearings held there were "so flimsy, so emotional, so unlegal," reported Howe, that he chose to resign rather than carry out the deportation orders. Hearings were conducted without lawyers or witnesses. Detectives served as prosecutor, witness, judge, and jailor. Hundreds of aliens were deported without a chance to defend themselves.

> Things that were done [Howe wrote] forced one almost to despair. The Department of Justice, the Department of Labor, and Congress not only failed to protest against hysteria, they encouraged these excesses; the State not only abandoned the liberty which it should have protected, it lent itself to the stamping out of individualism and freedom.

The Red Scare was out of control. Though President Wilson had appointed Howe personally, Howe's protests went unheard. When someone demanded that Howe himself be investigated as a Red for not ordering the deportations, he saw his choice and resigned.

On went the terror. Thirty-two states and many cities

passed laws making it a crime to display a red flag. A Socialist duly elected to Congress was denied his seat. Reelected, he was denied it again. Teachers were fired from their jobs for their opinions or made to sign loyalty oaths. Textbooks were purged of any radical taint. The anarchists' Modern School was investigated and denounced by a New York State committee. It was the school which, fulfilling her promise to herself, Emma and her friends had established back in 1910, on the model of the Paris Beehive school. "That such an institution should have been allowed to exist for almost ten years is not a very high compliment to the City of New York," reported the committee, and closed the school down. "Too many people in this country are enjoying the right of free speech," said a typical newspaper editorial, this one in the Brooklyn *Eagle*. It didn't matter that free speech was guaranteed in the Constitution.

It was almost midnight. Outside, a biting December wind cut through the air and deep snow covered the shores of Ellis Island. Emma was finishing up a few farewell letters when she heard footsteps outside her cell. "Someone's coming!" whispered one of her two cellmates. Quickly Emma hid her letters under her pillow and pretended to be asleep.

Two guards and a matron entered the room. "Get up. Get your things. Hurry!" they ordered. Emma hid her letters under a large shawl she wrapped around her.

The three women were marched to the large corridor where hundreds of male prisoners were standing around in confusion. Emma saw Sasha, already trying to establish some order among the men.

Suddenly federal agents filled the corridor. "Line up!" came the officer's order. Emma looked at her watch. It was 4:20 A.M.

Everyone fell silent and lined up. "March!" ordered the officer.

One by one, the 249 aliens marched onto a waiting barge, the three women last. The barge would take them through the December wind out to an old army transport waiting in the harbor. Left over from the Spanish-American War, the steamship *Buford*, nicknamed by the press the Red Ark, was expected to head for Russia.

Dawn was just breaking over New York's skyline as the first frightened prisoners boarded the barge. For many of them America was home—a home they would never see again. Twelve of them were being parted from their wives and children, who had been refused permission to accompany them. Most of the deportees had never participated in any terrorist activities. Most of them had no criminal records of any sort. They were being deported not for anything they had *done,* but rather for what they *believed.*

As Emma's eye scanned the New York skyline, she suddenly caught sight of the Statue of Liberty. How much Emma had learned since she had first glimpsed the statue in the harbor more than thirty years before. No longer did the Torch of Liberty burn for her. For all the poor passengers of the *Buford* the flame of liberty had long before gone out. When it went out for them, it went out all over America.

Emma was heartsick and exhausted. Still, she managed to make a fitting statement to the congressmen and reporters who had gathered in the cold dawn to cheer the *Buford* off. "I consider it an honor," she said with pride and defiance, "to be chosen as the first political agitator to be deported from the United States." It was certainly a distinction.

"Merry Christmas, Emma!" yelled one of the congressmen.

Abandoning for a moment her dignified stance, Emma glowered fiercely at the man; then, relaxing into her own favorite style, she mockingly thumbed her nose at him. It was the farewell he deserved.

There were four days left until Christmas, and a new year was coming. Emma looked hopefully ahead as the Red Ark steamed slowly out of the New York harbor and into the sea.

17

Russia: A Dream Betrayed

[They say] one can't make an omelette without breaking eggs. . . . I can see the broken eggs. Now where's this omelette of yours?
—THE POET PANAIT ISTRATI, ON THE BOLSHEVIK REVOLUTION, REPORTED BY VICTOR SERGE

In a crowded car of a sealed train, guarded by soldiers with bayonets, Emma and Sasha huddled together for warmth. The train was hurtling across icy Finland toward the Russian border. Though the border was still hours away, for Emma the discomfort was easy to bear. As soon as it was over, she would at long last be free. She was giddy with anticipation.

The ocean voyage on the leaky *Buford* had been even more uncomfortable than the sealed train. With only two toilets for the 249 prisoners, little food, damp and crowded quarters, and no freedom, there had been much illness and anger aboard. They had had a gloomy Christmas and an even gloomier New Year's. But as the end of the voyage approached, the prisoners' spirits began to lift. Most of them felt they were about to launch a new revolutionary life. At last they would be able to see their dreams in action. Nothing could keep them down.

Many years before, as a girl of sixteen, Emma had gone from Russia to America with high hopes for a fresh, free life. Her hopes had begun to crumble on the very first day. Now, as a woman of fifty, she was traveling back from America to Russia, her expectations of a free life firmer than ever before. She knew more now; she felt she was stronger and wiser than she had been at sixteen. It would take much more this time to crush her dreams.

When the Russian Revolution had erupted two years before, Emma had rushed to defend it. She had proclaimed the New Russia the "promise and the hope of the world." Now she would see the miracle for herself. She waited impatiently with the other prisoners.

At the border a reception committee of high government dignitaries waited on the Russian side to welcome the deportees. The moment the guards released the prisoners they all pushed eagerly out of the train.

Emma lagged behind. She had waited so long to set foot on revolutionary soil that she wanted the first moment all to herself. A lifetime dream was coming true. She was coming home at last—to the land of her birth and the land of the revolution. Choked with emotion, she stepped solemnly across the border into the New Russia.

Emma and Sasha were received in St. Petersburg, the grand city of Emma's childhood, with honors and deference. No longer were they hounded as criminals, as they had been in America. Here, where capitalism had been wiped out, they were treated with respect.

Nevertheless, almost as soon as they arrived Emma sensed that things were not as they should be. True, the people she met high up in the government were all full of enthusiasm for the revolution. Everyone worked, and bustled, and planned. Yet from the beginning, something struck Emma as wrong.

In her childhood, St. Petersburg had been lively and gay, even though it had reeked of poverty. Now a pall, an awful stillness, seemed to hang over the city. People in the streets were no less hungry or ill-clothed than they had been under the czar; only now they were silent besides. Emma was puzzled.

There were many discrepancies between what Emma had expected to see and what she saw in the land of the revolution. The Bolshevik officials who made up the new government had better food, better housing, better schools for their children, than everyone else. Instead of equal food for everyone, there were thirty-four different classes of food rations, with the best going to the highest officials. The death sentence had been abolished, yet each night volleys of gunfire pierced the air. The prisons had been thrown open, yet everywhere one looked there were police and prisoners. Prostitution had been officially ended, but wretched women solicited openly on the street. Special government permits and passes were needed for everything. People wasted their lives standing on endless numbers of endless lines.

When Emma attended a meeting of the Petro Soviet, the new governing body of the St. Petersburg area, she could hardly believe what she saw. Anyone faintly critical of the government was shouted down. All criticism was considered "counterrevolutionary," against the revolution. Dissent was not tolerated. The government with its police controlled everything.

Perhaps, thought Emma, in the new capital city of Moscow things would be better. Perhaps there were special reasons for the trouble in St. Petersburg. She and Sasha traveled to Moscow. They talked to the workers of Moscow and the women in the markets. Soon Emma saw the same abuses she had seen in St. Petersburg. Everywhere were hunger and privilege, bureaucracy and repression. "Communism, equality, freedom," jeered the women in the market—"lies and deception."

Emma could no longer silence her doubts. She began asking people she knew for explanations. No matter whom she asked, she always heard the same answers and excuses. Russia was still in the midst of a civil war, they told her. Mutinies broke out everywhere. The revolution was under attack from all sides. There was a terrible food and fuel shortage. The peasants could not produce enough food to feed the townspeople, and without food the workers in the towns could not keep the factories running. In desperation the government had to take food forcibly from the peasants to feed the workers, and it had to force the workers back to the factories. Otherwise the famine would increase. Extreme measures were necessary until the revolution was safe from its enemies.

What Emma's friends told her was true. Famine and disease had claimed seven million lives in the first two and a half years of Bolshevik rule. Armed enemies *were* attacking the revolutionary forces on all sides. Freedom *did* seem to be a luxury Russia could not yet afford. The head of the entire government, the great Lenin himself, told Emma that "there can be no free speech in a revolutionary period"; free speech, he said, was a middle-class notion. Protecting the revolution must come before *everything*. Not only Bolsheviks but even Sasha chided Emma for doubting the revolution.

Longing to see the revolution succeed, Emma tried to accept the explanations she was given. She was a newcomer, she told herself. She must try not to judge until she knew all the facts. "I held on to the firm belief that the Bolshevik [s] were our brothers in a common fight," she wrote. "Our very lives and all our revolutionary hopes were staked upon it." If there was a dictatorship, it was only temporary; at least it was a dictatorship of the workers. Freedom would come in time, when the crisis was past. She must not expect anarchism to rise all at once from the ruins of capitalism. First a new economic life had to be built throughout the entire land. Instead of finding fault, she told herself, she must find useful work to do. She must join the revolution, not doubt it.

With their great prestige in Russia, Emma and Sasha

were offered many jobs. But they could find none to suit them. Every job they were offered seemed to be under the direct control of the government. As anarchists, they refused to take orders from any government, even from a revolutionary one. They visited the aged Peter Kropotkin, by that time living in Russia too, and found him facing the same dilemma: whether to criticize the government or join it.

Finally Emma and Sasha were offered a job collecting historical documents for the new Museum of the Revolution. The job was not under direct government control, and it would take them all over Russia. They would be able to observe the revolution firsthand—in the country and the provinces—without officials to guide them.

They went to work. The museum expedition was given a special railroad car to make into a traveling home and office. Emma and Sasha furnished it with beds and cupboards, dishes and pots. In large letters across the side of the car they had painted: EXTRAORDINARY COMMISSION OF THE MUSEUM OF THE REVOLUTION. When they were all finished, they moved into their new rolling home with the other four members of the expedition. Hitching their car onto the first available train, they left Moscow for the provinces. Now they would see for themselves.

Everywhere they went, from Kharkov to Kiev, it was the same story. The more they traveled, the more disillusioned they became. Emma observed the government bureaucracy growing into a huge "Frankenstein monster." In the factories she inspected she saw workers forced at gunpoint to work under conditions more brutal than had existed under the czar. So what if they were producing "for the revolution"? Even in towns where there was food in the markets, she saw starving people staring into the windows of well-stocked shops. Everywhere political prisoners, many of them anarchists, filled the jails. Everywhere, police power and privilege were gaining control.

If the revolution had to support so much injustice and brutality, thought Emma, then what was its purpose? No ends could justify such terrible means.

In their farewell message written on Ellis Island, Emma and Sasha had urged the American people to

> resent injustice and every outrage on liberty. Demand an open mind and fair hearing for every idea. Hold sacred the right of expression: protect the freedom of speech and press. Suffer not Thought to be forcibly limited and opinions proscribed. Make conscience free, undisciplined. Allow no curtailment of aspirations and ideals.

Now Emma realized that her hopes for the revolution had made her forget her own warnings. True, the people of Russia were no longer crushed by the power of a handful of property-owners. But under the powerful Bolshevik government freedom, justice, anarchism, were only dreams. The masses of workers and peasants who had so eagerly fought for the revolution no longer had any voice at all in deciding policy. Whatever their genuine social gains, politically, it seemed, they had simply traded one set of masters for another. The monstrous State had taken over everything.

"Ah, the revolution—what has become of it?" said one worker after another. Of Emma's own revolutionary dreams nothing was left, she said, "but ashes."

By the spring of 1921, whatever doubts still lingered in Emma's mind about the "Bolshevik myth" were dispelled forever. Shortly after the special car of the Extraordinary Commission of the Museum of the Revolution returned to St. Petersburg, the workers and peasants of the area called a strike. Sixteen thousand sailors of nearby Kronstadt, led by anarchists, supported the strikers. The sailors had fought bravely in the revolutionary Red Navy back in 1917. These were the very sailors who had picketed the United States Embassy for Sasha, Mooney, and Billings. Now, together with the strikers, they drew up a message to the government naming their grievances. They asked for freedom of speech and press, freedom for peasants to control the land, democratic elections of officials, bread.

Immediately the government moved in to put down the strike by force, calling it a mutiny. The government could not allow its power to be challenged or criticized. Instead of discussing the workers' grievances, it sent armies to besiege the city of Kronstadt. Leon Trotsky, the chief of the Red Army, demanded total, unconditional surrender. "This is the last warning," he said gravely, as he moved twenty-seven rifle divisions on the city. Great guns made ready to fire.

Emma and Sasha were horrified at the coming slaughter. Why wouldn't the government try to settle the strike peacefully? How could they accuse the strikers and sailors of opposing the revolution? Trotsky himself had called the Kronstadt sailors "the pride and glory of the revolution."

Suddenly the truth flashed clear to Emma and Sasha: the iron arm of the government would never permit any opposition, not even from within. Rule by the people was simply part of the "Bolshevik myth."

In face of the approaching disaster, Emma and Sasha decided the time had come to take a stand. They could no longer look on silently. Knowing their protest would not be heeded, they nevertheless sent a strong message to the government: "Comrade Bolsheviks," they wrote, "bethink yourselves before it is too late. Do not play with fire. You are about to make a most serious and decisive step. Settle the dispute by peaceful means."

Their protest was ignored and the fire came. For ten days and nights government troops shelled the helpless city of Kronstadt, crushing Russia's last open demand for community rule. When the massacre was over, 18,000 people lay dead.

Emma and Sasha realized they must leave Russia at once, to "escape from the horrible revolutionary sham and pretense." Never again could they confuse the revolution with an institution like the Bolshevik State. They wanted to spend the rest of their lives serving the revolution, but they knew it would be impossible to do it "gagged and chained" in Russia.

They moved out of their government rooms as soon as they could, into a tiny, seedy apartment in Moscow. Without their government rations and privileges, they had to collect and chop their own firewood, lugging it miles through the snow and up three flights of stairs on their feeble backs. They had to fetch water twice a day from a long distance. They had to cook and wash everything themselves, like the poorest workers. Though they ached from the work and were in constant danger of arrest, all hardships seemed worth it. Their pain and exhaustion, said Emma, "were as nothing to our inner liberation." They felt free again—free of oppressive government ties and free of all illusions.

Once settled in Moscow, they sent a strong protest to the government denouncing the new persecutions of anarchists. Most of their friends had by then been thrown in jail; the anarchists' hatred of government was no longer tolerated. Their own apartment had been raided, but they themselves remained free, probably because of their fame abroad.

They applied for passports to leave Russia and sent messages to anarchists in western Europe that they were coming. Then they sat back and waited. During their last months in Russia, many of their old radical friends passed through Moscow. Usually the friends were among some visiting delegation of Americans or Frenchmen or Englishmen who had been invited to Russia by the government. Emma and Sasha tried to tell them the truth about the situation, but few of them listened. They still believed, as Emma no longer did, that the end justifies any means. In love with the revolution before they came, they saw only what they were shown and wanted to see. The American journalist Lincoln Steffens spoke for many western radicals when, after visiting Russia, he said: "I have been over into the future, and it works." To Emma and Sasha, who had lived there for two hideous years, it wasn't the future and it didn't work at all. In fact, in Emma's view, "the Russian Revolution—more correctly, Bolshevik methods—conclusively demonstrated how a revolution should *not* be made." Indeed, "the triumph of the [Bolshevik] State meant the defeat of the Revolution."

Just when the pair had decided to risk fleeing the country illegally, their passports arrived. On December 21, 1921, four days before Christmas, they boarded a train for Latvia. That day, Emma wrote, "One thought stood out in bold relief: I must raise my voice against the crimes committed in the name of the Revolution."

Two years after they had come to Russia, the "King and Queen of American anarchism" left, sick with disappointment, "desolate and denuded of dreams."

18

Exile

If you are among brigands and you are silent,
You are a brigand yourself.
                    —FROM AN OLD HUNGARIAN POEM

The exile of the anarchists did not end when they left
Russia. In some ways it was only beginning. No country
was willing to have them for more than a brief stay. In
Latvia they were thrown into jail and held in solitary
confinement until arrangements could be made for
them to leave the country. From Latvia they fled to Es-
tonia, then to Sweden, then to Germany, where they
were permitted to stay only from month to month. In
Bavaria they were first jailed, then expelled. They were
denied entrance to Norway and Denmark. Emma was
offered a visa for Austria on condition that she promise

to stay out of public life, but she refused indignantly. "Life as we live it today," she wrote to the English philosopher Bertrand Russell, "is not worth much. I would not feel it was worth anything if I had to foreswear what I believe and stand for."

Eventually the outcasts found homes, Sasha in Germany and Emma in England. Each wrote a book exposing to the world the horrors committed by the Bolshevik State in the name of communism and revolution. In her book *My Disillusionment in Russia* Emma expressed herself once and for all on the question of violence. It was a question that had troubled her since she had turned revolutionary at twenty. "That destruction and terror are part of revolution I do not dispute," she wrote in the preface.

> I have never denied that violence is inevitable nor do I gainsay it now. Yet it is one thing to employ violence in combat, as a means of defense. It is quite another thing to make a principle of terrorism, to institutionalize it. . . . Such terrorism begets counter-revolution and in turn becomes counter-revolutionary.

When Emma arrived in London in 1924, friends arranged a large dinner to introduce her to the city's radical circles. Hundreds of people turned out to meet her. When she rose to speak, she was welcomed with enthusiastic applause. When she sat down again, however, a deadly hush fell over the room. She had devoted her entire speech to criticizing Russia, and hardly a radical could be found in London willing to believe what she said. Emma's faith was in the revolution to come; theirs was still in the Russian Revolution that had already taken place. Eventually a good many English and American radicals would see through the claims of the Russian Revolution. Disillusioned and fearful, many of them, unlike Emma, would go so far as to abandon their radical vision altogether; sadly, some would even turn to persecuting revolutionaries. But in 1924 most of them would not permit anyone even to question Russia's achievement, not even Emma Goldman.

Being an outcast among friends was nothing new for Emma. Her fierce integrity had often landed her in that position before. Almost alone among anarchists she had worked to save the life of the assassin Czolgosz. Almost alone among feminists she had exposed the illusions about woman suffrage. Now, almost alone among radicals she denounced Bolshevism. "Censorship from comrades had the same effect on me as police persecution; it made me surer of myself," she once wrote. Now she set to work organizing protests against the Russian persecution of anarchists and other political prisoners. But only a handful of people supported her.

When Jim Colton, an old anarchist miner from Wales, offered to marry Emma, she did not dismiss his offer. She knew the English authorities would let her go on denouncing Bolshevik injustice or lecturing on the drama indefinitely. But she also knew that if she tried to denounce English injustice she would likely lose her visa. Hating to be censored and longing to be free, she decided to marry Colton. Married, she would be able to claim the rights of all British citizens: free speech and a valid passport. She paid Colton's fare from Wales to

London and back again, as well as his lost days' wages, and officially married the "old rebel," as she called him, in June 1925. "I can't thank dear, old, kindly Colton enough for it," she wrote to Sasha. After Colton returned to Wales, Emma, passport in hand, went off to France for a long holiday, then on to Canada for a year-long lecture tour.

The Canadian anarchist movement was almost dead when Emma arrived; it was on its way to recovery by the time she left. Traveling from city to city, she left a wide trail of converts. She lectured on birth control, literature, anarchism, Russia. She once stayed for fifteen lectures in a town where she had been scheduled to deliver only two. Sometimes she spoke three times a day. Canadian anarchists begged her to settle in Canada with them, even offering to support her.

But Emma had other things to do. For years her friends had been urging her to write her autobiography. So important did the project seem to them that they collected several thousand dollars for her to live on while she wrote the book. "Your life," the novelist Theodore Dreiser had told her, "is the richest of any woman's of the century." It had to be recorded.

In 1928 Emma retired to the tiny French fishing village of St. Tropez on the Mediterranean Sea to begin her book. She was fifty-nine years old. In a little cottage of three rooms, with an enchanting garden and an incomparable view of mountains and sea, she went to work. Sasha, too, was by then living in the south of France. For the next three years the old comrades once again worked side by side. "In bitter sorrow and ecstatic joy, in black despair and fervent hope," wrote Emma, "I had lived my life." Now, with Sasha to help her relive it, she would try to write it all down. If the book itself turned out to be the last chapter of her life, she would not complain. Her life had been full to overflowing, and she had "drunk the cup to the last drop."

When Emma emerged from her retreat in 1931 at age sixty-two, she found the world completely changed. Though her autobiography, *Living My Life,* was fairly well received, few people any longer had money to spend on books.

In 1929 the Great Depression hit every country in Europe and America, leaving them all economically devastated. People by the many millions were suddenly without jobs, food, shelter, hope. Governments were impotent and helpless; people felt they must resort to desperate measures. In one European nation after another people gave political support to whoever promised to pull the country out of the Depression. Some people viewed capitalism itself as the cause of the Depression. Many of them turned radical, hoping that some sort of worldwide socialism might solve the worldwide Depression. Other people placed their trust in tyrants, hoping that some powerful man or party might at least save their own nation. Few resisted as first Mussolini leading the Fascist Party in Italy, and then Hitler leading the Nazi Party in Germany, took control of their governments in the name of the fascist "revolution." Relying on popular feelings of national pride and patriotism, each fascist leader proclaimed the vast superiority of his own nation and race. Each promised to build an unshakable economy and a mighty nation for the masses of fellow Italians or Germans. Using military force, each made himself absolute dictator of his country, crushing all opposition and ruling by terror.

Emma saw the peril at once. Had she not spent her life warning against the dangers of concentrated political power? Now, as early as 1932, when Hitler's threats to conquer all Europe were still only words on paper, Emma set out to denounce "Hitler and his gang" everywhere she could. In 1932 she denounced him in Denmark, Norway, and Sweden. In 1933, after he had officially become dictator of Germany, she denounced him in England and in Holland. In 1934 she sailed to America to warn against him. First she spoke in Canada. By early spring certain distinguished friends had arranged permission for her to return to the United States for a ninety-day tour; then she denounced him in the United States.

Whenever she spoke out against fascism, embarrassed government officials, eager not to offend Hitler, tried to stop her. In Holland her meetings were canceled and she was expelled from the country. In the United States, after the German ambassador protested against her speeches to the State Department, she was issued a stern warning.

Emma's American tour was not a great success. After fifteen years' absence from the United States, she was received back as an interesting celebrity, but no more. Once feared as "the most dangerous woman in the world," she was no longer considered either a prophet or a threat. By the mid-thirties most people in the United States looked to strong central power as the only answer to the economic horrors of the Depression. Anarchist doctrine seemed obsolete. Franklin Delano Roosevelt, leading the Democratic Party, had been elected president in 1932 promising a New Deal for Americans. The New Deal depended on firm government control of the country's economic life. Radicals by the millions wanted even greater government control: they wanted the sort of State socialism Russia had. Many of them joined the American Communist Party to bring it about. With so many Americans newly radicalized by the horrors of the Depression, a new reaction of fear sprang up. Fascism, which was strongly anti-communist, became attractive to a good number of people. Between the communists, the New Dealers, and the fascists, all pursuing some form of strong central government, there was no room for Emma's ideal of local decentralized control. Once again, individual liberty seemed something of a luxury; anarchist ideas seemed irrelevant or soft or silly. Members of the Communist Party angrily boycotted Emma's lectures; other groups were not particularly interested. Emma's notions seemed hopelessly out of date.

Introducing an article of Emma's in the December 1934 issue of *Harper's Magazine,* the editors of *Harper's* said: "A generation ago it seemed to many American conservatives as if the opinions which Emma Goldman was expressing might sweep the world. Now she fights almost alone for what seems a lost cause." Nevertheless, the editors felt obliged to add: "her opinions are not ours."

The main point of the *Harper's* article—perhaps even Emma's purpose for writing it—was to warn America against accepting any authoritarian solution.

> Americans are so easily hoodwinked by the sanctity of law and authority. . . . Those in authority have and always will abuse their power. And the instances when they do not do so are as rare as roses growing on icebergs. . . . It is my conviction that dictatorship, whether to the right or to the left, can never work.

But it would take much more than Emma's voice to rouse the world to resist the turn to authority. Few people recognized the danger.

After her ninety days were up, Emma returned to Canada and wrote to Sasha in France to expect her. In May 1935, depressed and almost out of money, she sailed for France.

Her British passport enabled Emma to travel practically anywhere. Sasha, however, was tolerated only in France. Even in France, the government authorities had harassed him for years, not even allowing him to leave his village without permission. They only stopped when a committee of such distinguished scientists, writers, and philosophers as Albert Einstein, John Dewey, Thomas Mann, and Bertrand Russell petitioned the French government to leave Sasha alone.

Now ill, poor, unable to find enough work to live,

and growing old, Sasha welcomed Emma's return to France. The exiles needed each other.

"Men have come and gone in my long life. But you my dearest will remain forever," Emma wrote to Sasha on his sixty-fifth birthday. And he, addressing her still as his "immutable Sailor Girl," affirmed to Emma that their life together, spanning forty-five years, was for him "one of the most beautiful and rarest things in the world."

Forty-five years was indeed a very long time. The comrades had lived what seemed like many lives together. When Sasha died on June 28, 1936, the day after Emma's sixty-seventh birthday, Emma suffered the most painful loss of her life. Sasha's death, as she wrote to her niece Stella, was a "crushing weight . . . pressing down on my heart." Whenever in the long past she had felt most completely alone, she had always, somewhere, had "my pal Sasha." Even during his long imprisonment she had counted on his love. "My dear," she wrote in a note to him two days before his death, "I keep thinking what a long time to live. For whom? For what?" Their answer, she implied, was for each other.

Now, with the anarchist ideal seemingly "a lost cause," as the *Harper's* editors had said, and with her beloved Sasha gone, the old answer was no longer any good. "For whom? For what?" From now on she would have only herself and a dying cause to live for.

Or so it seemed. Then suddenly, less than two months later, her life was unexpectedly infused with a new, compelling purpose. Suddenly she was summoned to Spain to join the only people in all Europe who were actively resisting fascism. And they were resisting it with their very lives.

The people were the Spanish anarchists, fighting alongside socialists, communists, and even capitalists in a Popular Front against fascism. They were rushing to arms and to the barricades. And it was she, Emma Goldman, whom they needed.

19

Spain: A Dream Destroyed

I had dropped more or less by chance into the only community of any size in Western Europe where political consciousness and disbelief in capitalism were more normal than their opposites. . . . Many of the normal motives of civilized life —snobbishness, money-grubbing, fear of the boss, etc.—had simply ceased to exist.

—GEORGE ORWELL

Fresh from her mourning, Emma had gone to Spain to join in the fight against fascism. Though she knew that anarchism was deeply rooted in the Spanish soil, she never dreamed that in the middle of a bloody civil war against fascism, a mighty social revolution would be taking place.

In July 1936 four Spanish generals, headed by General Franco, had led the Spanish army in a fascist revolt to take over the government. Even before the weak republican government of Spain could decide what to do, the working people had demanded arms and started to

fight the fascist troops. The Spaniards were the only people in Europe who took up arms against fascism, but not before Franco had seized about half the land of Spain. It was the beginning of a long and terrible civil war.

On one side were the fascists, including the army, the Church, and the nobility. On the other side were all sorts of people. There were anarchists and socialists. There were the communists, who wanted a Spanish government modeled on Russia's. There were the middle-class republican supporters of Spain's moderate capitalist government. All these groups—sometimes called "loyalists" because they were "loyal" to the Spanish government—joined together in a Popular Front to defeat the fascists. It was this Popular Front that Emma rushed to Spain to join.

But when she arrived in Barcelona in September 1936 she was met by an amazing spectacle. There in war-torn Spain the revolution of her dreams had apparently sprung to life. Emma could hardly believe her eyes. Not only had the brave Spanish workers united to stop fascism; they had evidently united to end capitalism as well. Not only was capitalism being overthrown, but this revolution, unlike Russia's, was being made by anarchists. *This* was the revolution that could serve, Emma said, as a "shining example to the rest of the world." It was a popular revolution—a people's revolution. And it seemed to be working.

The spirit of revolution hung in the Barcelona air. The Barcelona workers, mostly anarchists, were in charge of the city. The gas, electrical, water, telephone, and public transportation services; the factories, trades, and small shops; the barbers, bootblacks, and waiters— all had organized themselves into collectives and had enlisted in the revolution. No one called anyone "sir" or "señor"; everyone was "comrade." The waiters in the restaurants, the clerks in the shops, even the bootblacks who shined the shoes, were all treated as equals. In the barbershops signs advised that they were now collectives, and that barbers were "no longer slaves." All tipping was abolished as demeaning. The bakers' collective of Barcelona vowed that as long as they had flour to knead, the population would have bread.

On the avenues, posters proclaimed that prostitutes were freed forever from the need to sell their bodies. "An anarchist," it was declared, "must not purchase kisses; he should merit them." Women, proclaiming their freedom, trained in militias like men. Divorce and marriage, always before in the Church's control, were made available on demand to any couple who wanted them.

The red and black flag of the Spanish anarchists flew from every large building in Barcelona. Prisons were "liberated" and the prisoners set free. The luxury hotels were taken over for headquarters of revolutionary committees and for feeding-stations. Streetcars and taxis were painted red and black. The boxes of the bootblacks were painted red and black. Revolutionary songs, blaring from loudspeakers, were taken up by the people in the streets. People everywhere greeted one another with the clenched fist, the gesture of the revolution. No one looked rich and no one looked destitute. With unemployment effectively eliminated, there were hardly any beggars; and if the rich still lived in Barcelona, they stayed off the streets. The Church, hated by Spanish anarchists, was stripped of its power and churches were destroyed. Anyone connected with the Church who had not fled from the city stayed out of sight.

Eager to serve the revolution, Emma accepted the job of directing the anarchist press, propaganda, and public information service in England. It was what she was best at, and it was a job that desperately needed to be done. If fascism was to be defeated in Spain, people elsewhere in Europe had to be roused to aid the Popular Front. People had to be convinced that harm would come to them if they sat by and allowed still another fascist victory. The Spanish people were giving their lives fighting fascism; the least the other countries must do was to give them money and arms.

If Emma were to convince the British, she needed to know firsthand what was really happening in Spain. She needed to know what kind of help was needed. She visited the factory collectives that had been taken over by the unions. Unlike those she had visited in Russia, which were run under orders from above, these factories were actually being run by the workers themselves and with amazing success. As long as there were raw materials, the factories could turn out products. But without foreign supplies, they would soon run out of raw materials.

Emma visited the countryside in the province of Aragon. There, in village after village, the peasants had collectivized the land and launched campaigns to wipe out illiteracy and disease. Many villages had abolished money as unnecessary, since everyone worked and people got what they needed from the village communal storehouse. In much of rural Spain, wrote the historian George Woodcock, "for the first time in living memory . . . there was work and food, if not luxury, for all. Land that had gone untilled for generations was cultivated again and no man starved." Spain's major economic problem had long been land reform. The land had been owned by powerful men who controlled enormous estates. Now, in a matter of months, the problem was on the way to being licked. Collectivization was apparently working.

Emma went to the Aragon battlefront where the worst fighting was going on. Separate army units of anarchists, of communists, of socialists, called "militias," were fighting side by side against the fascists. The militias had somehow achieved what was considered a military miracle: the miracle of equality. Boys of fifteen and sixteen fought as equals alongside their elders; soldiers were the equals of officers; even some women fought side by side with men. George Orwell, the English writer who went to Spain as a reporter and joined up to fight as a soldier, described the miracle of the militias:

> Everyone from general to private drew the same pay, ate the same food, wore the same clothes, and mingled on terms of complete equality. . . . There was no military rank in any ordinary sense; no titles, no badges, no heel-clicking and saluting. . . . There was a nearer approach to [equality] than I had ever seen or than I would have thought conceivable in time of war.

Eventually, as the war dragged on, the militias would all be joined together into a united People's Army. And eventually they would become like an ordinary army, losing their special heady spirit of equality. At the time Emma saw them, however, they were still operating out of revolutionary loyalty rather than out of military discipline based on fear. The only thing they seemed to lack was arms, and arms they needed desperately. Emma would try to obtain them.

By the time Emma had toured Spain she was more than ever convinced that this anarchist revolution was working. How different it all was from the revolution in Russia. That one had been a sham; this one was the real thing. "Your revolution," she said to a mass meeting of anarchist youth, "will destroy forever [the notion] that anarchism stands for chaos."

Unfortunately, the social revolution was not the only thing happening in Spain. There was a civil war against fascism going on besides. To Emma there was only one war in the world worth fighting. That was the revolution against capitalism—not a nation's war but a people's war. Here in Spain, however, the people's war against capitalism and the government's war against fascism were all bound up together. Clearly, the revolution could survive only if the fascists were defeated. But just as clearly, the fascists could never be defeated by the anarchists alone. To win the war against fascism the anarchists would have to join with their natural enemies. They would have to join with the communists, who were already trying to gain control of the Popular Front government, and with the republicans, who were against all revolutions. The situation was not at all simple; the best policy was not at all clear.

The anarchists' policy was, in the words of one of their slogans, "make war and the revolution at the same time." The communists, whose idea of revolution was to nationalize industry and place it under State control, thought it best to "win the war first and make the revolution afterwards." And the republicans wanted to win the war and prevent the revolution altogether.

In fact, the anarchists faced a painful dilemma. They had to decide whether to oppose the government as the principles and spirit of anarchism demanded, or to compromise their principles by collaborating with the government. If they opposed the government, they would destroy antifascist unity. If they joined the government they would be strengthening the very parties and institutions that wanted to destroy anarchism. It was a terrible choice to have to make, so terrible that the revolution might not be able to survive it.

Whatever the Spanish anarchists decided, Emma vowed to do her utmost to help them. Filled with the enthusiasm and inexhaustible energy of a young woman, at sixty-seven she returned to England to do the job assigned her. She felt as though her life were beginning all over again.

In England she wrote articles, made speeches, published an English edition of the Spanish anarchists' journal, formed committees, organized letter-writing campaigns to the press. She did everything possible to aid the Spanish anarchists. But her work did little good. For though people feared fascism, they evidently feared the revolution more. There was a campaign of silence against the Spanish revolution in the European press that made Emma's job almost impossible. Newspapers refused to print stories that acknowledged that a revolution was going on in Spain. Instead they pretended that the battle in Spain was only between fascism and capitalist democracy. This lie made it hard to rouse European radicals to help.

The European democratic governments did almost nothing to help Spain either. They were too frightened of revolution. Italy and Germany were openly supplying the fascists in Spain with weapons and troops. But only Russia gave arms to the antifascist side. As a result, the communists of Spain, with close ties to Russia, started gaining power far beyond their numbers. Simply by threatening to withhold arms, the Russians, through the Spanish Communist Party, were able to control the policy of the Spanish government.

Soon after Emma joined them, the Spanish anarchists, against all their principles, made the painful decision to join the Popular Front government. Hoping to influence policy and promote unity, they accepted four cabinet posts. For the sake of the war effort they traded their revolutionary spirit for the spirit of compromise. From that time on, Emma pointed out, they were working for their enemies.

Before long, the communists, in control of the government, were openly sabotaging anarchist achievements. The anarchist-run factories were taken over by the government, in the name of a united war effort. Anarchist soldiers at the front were refused arms. The anarchists' agricultural collectives that were not de-stroyed by fascist troops were destroyed by communist troops.

Emma, writing in the journal *Spain and the World,* observed:

> From the moment [anarchist leaders] entered into ministries and submitted to the conditions imposed upon them by Soviet Russia in return for some arms, I foresaw the inevitable price our comrades will have to pay. . . . The Anarchist participation in the Government and the concessions made to Russia have resulted in almost irreparable harm to the Revolution.

Emma did not approve of the anarchists' compro-mises, but she understood their painful dilemma. She wrote to her friend Ethel Mannin:

> Having come close to the insurmountable difficulties confronting the [anarchists] I can understand better the concessions they have made and are making. I can-not reconcile myself to some of them, but I realize that when one is in a burning house one does not consider one's possessions, one tries to jump to safety.

The tension between anarchists and communists mounted steadily in the early months of 1937. On May 3 they reached a terrible bloody climax. Government forces, mainly communist, tried to seize the Telephone Exchange building in Barcelona. That building had been occupied and run by anarchists since the very be-ginning of the war. The anarchists resisted. Gun fights and rioting broke out in the streets of Barcelona, lasting for days. Anarchists and communists killed each other while General Franco's fascists sat quietly by preparing to win the war.

It was probably then that the anarchist revolution was irrevocably doomed in Spain. Emma wrote in an article: "The glorious achievements of the [anarchists] have received a terrible jolt. I fear very much that [they] will not recover from it so soon." By then it was clear to Emma that whether communists or fascists won the war, the anarchists would lose.

It would be a terrible loss. "It is as though you had wanted a child all your life, and at last, when you had almost given up hoping, it had been given to you—only to die soon after it was born," Emma wrote to a friend.

And still, she continued to pour all her energy into the Spanish struggle. In October 1938 she attended a congress of Spanish anarchist workers and youth. Once again, on the eve of defeat, the idealistic anarchists debated their fundamental principles. By then it was too late for anything to save them, least of all a return to first principles. In January 1939 Franco's troops entered Barcelona, always the main stronghold of anarchism in Spain, the city of the revolution. Barcelona fell to Franco without a struggle. The child that was Emma's dream died in its sleep.

20

A Fitting End

*Real generosity toward the future lies in giving
all to the present.*

—ALBERT CAMUS

Even after the revolution was clearly lost, Emma went
to Canada to raise funds for Spain. She could not give
up. On the verge of a second catastrophic World War,
the whole world, not only Spain, was in danger of suc-
cumbing to fascism. If there was still something—
anything—left to do, Emma wanted to do it. "I am
more than ever [determined]," she had said to friends
some few years earlier, "that my life should end as it
began, fighting." If her life sometimes looked like an
endless series of defeats, it was because she always chose
to fight the most difficult battles.

On February 17, 1940, still in Canada, the seventy-year-old Emma suffered a stroke. Three months later, on May 14, she died.

"If I had my life to live over again," she had written in an article in *Harper's,* "like anyone else, I should wish to alter minor details. But in any of my more important actions and attitudes I would repeat my life as I have lived it."

She had lived as she had chosen to live, and now she died as she had chosen to die. Both, she did splendidly.

Once, many years before, Emma had placed a wreath of flowers on the grave of the Haymarket martyrs in Chicago. Over the grave stood a monument to the martyred Anarchists: a figure of a woman who with one hand places a crown on a dying man, and with her other hand draws a dagger. To Emma the woman seemed to express "defiance and revolt, mingled with pity and love." The woman's face was "beautiful in its great humanity"; her gesture was "infinite tenderness."

With such qualities, the figure might have stood for Emma herself.

In accordance with her wishes, Emma's body was buried in Chicago's Waldheim Cemetery near the graves of the revered Haymarket martyrs, the "precious dead" who had inspired her life. It was a fitting end. The monument to those anarchists buried in Chicago would now serve for Emma as well.

Selected Bibliography

Works by Emma Goldman

Anarchism and Other Essays. New York: Dover Books, 1970.

Living My Life. New York: Alfred A. Knopf, 1931. (Dover Books, paperback reprint, 2 vols., 1970.)

My Disillusionment in Russia. New York: Thomas Y. Crowell Company (Apollo paperback ed.), 1970.

The Social Significance of the Modern Drama. Boston: Richard G. Badger, 1914.

Works About Emma Goldman

DELL, FLOYD. *Women as World Builders: Studies in Modern Feminism,* Ch. V. Chicago: Forbes and Co., 1913.

DRINNON, RICHARD. *Rebel in Paradise.* Chicago: Univ. of Chicago Press, 1961.

HARRIS, FRANK. "Emma Goldman" in *Contemporary Portraits,* 4th series, pp. 223–251. New York: Brentano's, 1923. (Reprinted in Apollo ed. of *My Disillusionment in Russia.*)

HAVEL, HIPPOLYTE. "Biographical Sketch" in Emma Goldman's *Anarchism and Other Essays.*

ISHILL, JOSEPH. *Emma Goldman: A Challenging Rebel.* Berkeley Heights, N.J.: Oriole Press, 1957.

MANNIN, ETHEL. *Women and the Revolution.* New York: E. P. Dutton, 1939.

WEST, REBECCA. Introduction to Emma Goldman's *My Disillusionment in Russia.*

Works About Anarchism

BAKUNIN, MICHAEL. *The Political Philosophy of Bakunin: Scientific Anarchism.* Ed. by G. P. Maximoff. Glencoe, Ill.: The Free Press (paperback ed.), 1964.

BERKMAN, ALEXANDER. *Now and After: The ABC of Communist Anarchism.* New York: Vanguard Press, 1929.

GOODMAN, PAUL. *People or Personnel.* New York: Random House (Vintage paperback ed.), 1968.

HOROWITZ, IRVING L., ed. *The Anarchists.* New York: Dell Publishing Co., 1964.

JACKER, CORINNE. *The Black Flag of Anarchism.* New York: Charles Scribner's Sons, 1968.

JOLL, JAMES. *The Anarchists.* New York: Grosset and Dunlap (Universal Library paperback ed.), 1966.

KORNBLUH, JOYCE L., ed. *Rebel Voices: An I.W.W. Anthology.* Ann Arbor, Mich.: Univ. of Michigan Press, 1964.

KROPOTKIN, PETER. *Mutual Aid.* Boston: Extending Horizons Press, 1970.

PROUDHON, PIERRE-JOSEPH. *Selected Writings.* Ed. by Stewart Edwards. Garden City, N.Y.: Doubleday & Co. (Anchor paperback ed.), 1969.

RUSSELL, BERTRAND. *Proposed Roads to Freedom.* New York: Barnes & Noble (paperback ed.), 1965.

WOODCOCK, GEORGE. *Anarchism: a History of Libertarian Ideas and Movements*. Cleveland: World Publishing Co. (Meridian paperback ed.), 1962.

Works on Important Events in Emma Goldman's Life

On Russia During Emma Goldman's Childhood

GORKY, MAXIM. *Autobiography*. New York: Citadel Press, 1969.

KROPOTKIN, PETER. *Memoirs of a Revolutionist*. New York: Grove Press (Evergreen paperback ed.), 1970.

VENTURI, FRANCO. *Roots of Revolution*. New York: Grosset & Dunlap (Universal Library paperback ed.), 1966.

WIRTH, LOUIS. *The Ghetto*. Chicago: Univ. of Chicago Press, 1928.

On the Haymarket Affair

DAVID, HENRY. *The History of the Haymarket Affair*. New York: Collier Books (paperback ed.), 1963.

On the Homestead Steel Strike and the Assault on Frick

BERKMAN, ALEXANDER. *Prison Memoirs of an Anarchist*. New York: Mother Earth Publishing Assoc., 1912.

DAVID, HENRY. "Upheaval at Homestead" in *America in Crisis,* ed. by Daniel Aaron. New York: Alfred A. Knopf, 1952.

On the Assassination of President McKinley

DONOVAN, ROBERT J. *The Assassins,* Ch. IV. New York: Harper & Bros., 1955.

LEECH, MARGARET. *In the Days of McKinley*. New York: Harper & Bros., 1959.

On the "Woman Question"

DITZION, SIDNEY. *Marriage, Morals, and Sex in America*. New York: Octagon Books, 1970.

FLEXNER, ELEANOR. *Century of Struggle*. New York: Atheneum (paperback ed.), 1968.

O'NEILL, WILLIAM L., ed. *The Woman Movement: Feminism in the United States and England*. New York: Barnes & Noble, 1969.

On the Red Scare

GENTRY, CURT. *Frame-up: the Incredible Case of Tom Mooney and Warren Billings*. New York: W. W. Norton & Co., 1967.

HOWE, FREDERIC C. *The Confessions of a Reformer*. New York: Charles Scribner's Sons, 1925 (Chicago: Quadrangle paperback ed., 1967).

MURRAY, ROBERT K. *Red Scare: A Study of National Hysteria, 1919–1920*. New York: McGraw-Hill Book Co. (paperback ed.), 1964.

On Revolutionary Russia

BALABANOFF, ANGELICA. *My Life as a Rebel*. New York: Harper & Bros., 1938.

BERKMAN, ALEXANDER. *The Bolshevik Myth*. New York: Boni & Liveright, 1925.

REED, JOHN. *Ten Days That Shook the World*. New York: Mentor Books, 1967.

On the Spanish Civil War

BRENAN, GERALD. *The Spanish Labyrinth*. New York: The Macmillan Company, 1943.

ORWELL, GEORGE. *Homage to Catalonia*. Boston: Beacon Press (paperback ed.), 1955.

THOMAS, HUGH. *The Spanish Civil War*. New York: Harper & Row (Colophon paperback ed.), 1963.

Index

ILLUSTRATIONS FOLLOW PAGE 98.

agricultural collectives, Spanish, 232
Albany Law Journal, 43
Alexander II, Czar, assassination of, 23, 67, 115
Alexander III, Czar, 24
Alien Exclusion Act, 192
aliens, hysteria against German, 188-189
Amalgamated Iron and Steel Workers of America strike, 78, 80-81
  H. C. Frick assassination attempt and, 87
American Protective League, World War I and, 189
anarchism:
  Bolshevik government and, 207
  in Canada, 217

anarchism (*cont.*)
  description of, 50-51
  differences within, 74, 88-89
  education and, 140-141
  fear of in America, 123, 125, 126
  human nature and, 51-53
  Paris and, 112
  social institutions and, 96-97
  violence and, 59-61
  women and, 112, 162-163
Anarchist Exclusion Act (1903), 126-129
  Emma Goldman's test case of, 128-129
anarchists:
  conventions of, 111, 112, 139-140, 162-163

anarchists (cont.)
  deportation of, 192, 194-
    196, 200-202
  labor union of, 146
  mass hysteria against, 43-
    44, 123, 190-192, 196-
    200
  panic of 1893 and, 93-
    94
  police harassment of, 138,
    144-145
  Preparedness Parade and,
    176-178
  public cruelty to, 123
  in Russia, 49, 209, 210,
    212
  Spanish Civil War and,
    224-233
  violence stigma and, 42-
    44, 61, 176-178
  war and, 175
Anarchist Squad, Emma
  Goldman's harassment
  by, 138
anti-authoritarianism, Emma
  Goldman on, 221
Antiradical Division, U.S.
  Department of Justice,
  191-192, 196
anti-Semitism, 4-5, 6, 128
antiwar protests, see pacifists
Aragon, Emma Goldman in,
  227-228

arrests:
  Alexander Berkman's, 181
  Emma Goldman's, 92, 95-
    98, 108-109, 123-124,
    138, 170-171, 181
arts, "Progressive Era" and,
  131
assassination, 23-24, 27, 116
  attempted, 77, 81-88, 115
  Emma Goldman's evalua-
    tion of, 115-117
  of William McKinley, 120-
    127
  of other presidents, 119
Autonomie, Emma Gold-
  man and, 74-75

Bakunin, Michael:
  followers of, 67, 74
  Karl Marx and, 57
  on power, 56
  prison and, 102, 103
  violence and, 60
Bakunin, Tatiana, 103
Baldwin, Roger, 110
Barcelona, description of
  revolutionary, 225-227
Beehive school, anarchic
  principles of, 140-141,
  200
Berkman, Alexander, 75,
  103
  death of, 222

Berkman, Alexander (*cont.*)
deportation of, 195, 197, 198
description of, 66, 68
Emma Goldman and, 66-67, 71-72, 135-138, 222
escape plan of, 111, 114
French harassment of, 221-222
H. C. Frick, attempted assassination of, 81-88
imprisonment of, 92, 111, 114-115, 187, 194
politics of, 68-69, 158
Preparedness Parade bombing and, 175-177
Ben Reitman and, 149
resurgence of, 139
revisits Russia, 204-213
trials of, 90-92, 181-184
Billings, Warren:
defense committee for, 178, 185
frameup of, 177
Bill of Rights:
IWW defense of, 152
majority power and, 54
birth control, Emma Goldman and, 113, 168-171, 217
Black Friday, 45-46, 71
Blackwell's Island Penitentiary, 98-103

Blast (San Francisco), 175-177
alien expulsion and, 192
raid on, 176, 181
Bly, Nellie, 96-97
Bolshevik government:
Emma Goldman on, 205-213, 225
World War I withdrawal of, 189
Bolshevik Party, Russian Revolution and, 186
Bolshevik Revolution, betrayal of, 205-213
bombs:
Emma's reevaluation of, 116-117
experimentation with, 81
Haymarket affair and, 42-43
Preparedness Parade and, 175-176
boycotts, 59-60
Brady, Edward:
Emma Goldman and, 92-93, 103, 111, 159
prison and, 102
Brady, Mrs. E. G., as Emma Goldman's pseudonym, 106
brothel, Emma Goldman in, 85-86, 100
Buford, U.S.S., 188, 201-202

Buwalda, William, 151-152, 155

Canada, anarchist movement in, 217
capitalism:
   communism versus, 56-57
   economic inequality and, 55-56
Carnegie Steel Company, strike against, 78, 80-81
censorship, Russian, 24
Chekhov, Anton, 133
Chicago:
   Emma Goldman in, 121-125, 144-148
   Emma Goldman's grave in, 235
   lack of free speech in, 148
Church, the, in Barcelona revolution, 226-227
citizenship, Emma Goldman's, 141-143
Cleaver, Eldridge, 99
Cleveland, Grover, and women's roles, 167
cloakmakers' strike of 1889, 75
coal miners' strike, Pennsylvanian, 128
collectives:
   anarchist, 58
   in Barcelona, 225-227

Colton, Jim, 216-217
Cominski, Stella, see Stella Cominsky
commune, Emma Goldman's, 72-73, 75
communism, 56-57
communists (see also entries under Bolshevik):
   Spanish Civil War and, 225, 229, 231-233
communities, anarchist, 57-58
Conquest of Bread, The (Peter Kropotkin), 58
conscription, protest against, 179-180
conspiracy:
   antidraft movement viewed as, 179, 181-183, 186
   definition of, 182, 186
   Goldman-Berkman trial for, 181-184 186
   Justice John Harlan on, 714
Constitution, government power and, 54
contraceptives, 113, 168-171
Cossacks, pogroms by, 5
Criticism, New, 131
Czolgosz, Leon, 119-128, 195, 216

Darrow, Clarence, 129
decentralization, anarchism and, 57-58
democracies, anarchism versus, 53
demonstrations, 60
for Thomas Mooney, 177-178
Panic of 1893 and, 93-94
women's, 75
Dewey, John, 221
"direct action," versus voting, 59-60
discrimination, sexual, 172
divorce:
in Barcelona, 226
Emma Goldman's, 62
women's oppression and, 164
domination, anarchism versus, 52
Dostoyevsky, Feodor, 133
double standard, women's oppression and, 164-165, 172
Draft Bill, 179-186
drama:
New, 131, 132
Russian, 133
Dreiser, Theodore, 217
drinking, Emma Goldman's public, 168
Drinnon, Richard, 194

dynamitings, anarchist, 61
Eagle (Brooklyn), 200
economic control, capitalist, 54-55
economic inequality, 55
education, 140-141
"eight-hour day," Haymarket Affair and, 42
Einstein, Albert, 221
Elbe, S.S., 33
Ellis Island:
alien imprisonment on, 188
deportations from, 196, 199
Emerson, Ralph Waldo, 49
equality, myth of, 38-39, 55
executions, Bolshevik, 205
Extraordinary Commission of the Museum of the Revolution, 210
factory work, 28, 36-38
farm, Emma Goldman's, 137
fascism:
anti-communism of, 220
Emma Goldman's attacks on, 219-220
Spanish Civil War and, 225
Fascist Party (Italy), 218
FBI (Federal Bureau of Investigation), 191-192

February Revolution, *see* Russian Revolution
Federal Bureau of Investigation (FBI), 191-192
Fedya, comrade and lover of Emma Goldman, 72, 75-76, 80, 105
feminists:
definition of, 162
Emma Goldman and, 162-173
Fitzgerald, Eleanor, 175, 184
force, anarchism versus, 52
founding fathers, and suspicion of government, 54
France, anarchists in, 49
Franco, Francisco, 225, 233
free love, 161-163
Free Society (Chicago), 122
free speech:
ban on, 152-153
Emma Goldman's fight for, 145
lack of, 148, 151
myth of, 44
Free Speech League, 151
Anarchist Exclusion Act and, 129
Freiheit, 66
Emma Goldman and, 45, 47, 65, 69
Freud, Sigmund, 106, 132

Frick, Henry Clay:
attempted assassination of, 77, 81-86, 136
description of, 78
Homestead strike and, 78, 86

Garfield, James A., 119
Garson, Mr. (factory owner), 37-39
Genesis (book of the Bible), 158
German aliens:
hysteria against, 188-189
imprisonment of, 188
German National Socialist Workers Party (Nazi Party), 218
German socialist club (Rochester, N.Y.), 39-40
Germany:
Nazi Party in, 218
Spanish Civil War and, 231
ghettos, 4
St. Petersburg's, 24-25
God (*see also* religion), Emma Goldman's view of, 109
Goldman, Abraham, 18
caprice of, 31
cruelty of, 16-17

Goldman, Abraham (*cont.*)
dislike of Emma by, 1-2,
7, 159-160
Emma's birth and, 1-3
Emma's education and, 13
as innkeeper, 5-7
in St. Petersburg, 25-26
temperament of, 12
Goldman, Emma:
becomes anarchist, 47-48,
61-63
birth of, 1-2
childhood of, 1-33
conspiracy trial of, 181-
184, 186
death of, 235
deportation of, 194-195,
198, 200-202
education of, 13-20, 26-
28
exile of, 214-222
H. C. Frick assassination
attempt and, 81-93
"Home for Lost Dogs" of,
130-133
immigration to America
of, 32-35
imprisonment of, 98-103,
187, 194
marriages of, 40-41, 62,
216-217
revisits Russia, 204-213

Goldman, Helena, 2, 18
immigration to America
of, 32-33
reaction to injustice by,
10-11
in Rochester, N.Y., 35-36
solidarity with Emma of,
7, 16, 25, 30-31, 62-63
Goldman, Herman, 8
Goldman, Lena, 2, 18
immigration to America
of, 25
dislike of Emma by, 7-8
in Rochester, N.Y., 35-36
Goldman, Morris, 8
Goldman, Taube, 2, 18, 26,
193
border crossing and, 21-22
Emma's birth and, 2-3
oppression of, 8
Gorky, Maxim, 11
government:
anarchism versus, 50-53
distrust of, 54-55
government relief, 94-95
panic of 1893 and, 93-94
Great Depression, reaction
to, 218-220
Greenwich Village (New
York), 131
Gymnasium (Koenigsberg),
19-20

Hall, A. Oakey, 97
Hardwick, Thomas W., 190
Harlan, John M., 174
Harper's Magazine, 220-222
Harris, Frank, 163-164
Hauptmann, Gerhart, 106
Havel, Hippolyte, 112-114, 121, 130
  Mother Earth and, 139
Haymarket Affair, 49, 235
  effect on Emma Goldman of, 44-48, 71
  explanation of, 41-44, 67
  fear of anarchists and, 123
  labor movement and, 60
hierarchy, anarchism versus, 51-53
Hitler, Adolf, 218-219
Hobbes, Thomas, 51
hobos:
  anarchists and, 145-147
  description of, 145-146
  free speech and, 152
Holmes, Mr., hotel manager, 153, 155
Homestead strike, 78, 80-81
  H. C. Frick assassination attempt and, 87
Hoover, J. Edgar, 192, 194-195
Howe, Frederick, 199

Hugo, Victor, 21
Hunter Island (Pelham Bay, N.Y.), 132

Ibsen, Henrik, 106, 132
immigrants:
  New, 131
  treatment of, 36-39
immigration authorities, 141-143
International Anarchist Congress (Amsterdam), 139-140
International Anarchist Congress (Paris), 111, 112
  women's oppression and, 162-163
International Workers of the World (IWW), 146, 192
  free speech and, 152
  maltreatment of, 189, 197
Island of Tears, *see* Ellis Island
Istrati, Panait, 203
Italy:
  anarchists in, 49
  assassination of king of, 116
  Fascist Party in, 218
  Spanish Civil War and, 231

IWW, *see* International Workers of the World

Jackson, Andrew, 119
Jacobs, Detective, 95-98
jail, *see* prison
jealousy, anarchism and, 76
Jewish culture, women's place in, 159-160
Jews:
America and, 25, 35
anti-Semitism and, 4-6
in czarist Russia, 3
czar's assassination and, 24
pogroms against, 5, 25, 128
restrictions against, 18
job discrimination, women and, 172
justice, Haymarket Affair and, 43-45
Justice, U.S. Department of, Antiradical Division of, 191-192, 196

Kazin, Alfred, 131
Kershner, Jacob
citizenship of, 142-143, 194
marriage of, 40-41, 62
Kronstadt sailors:
Alexander Berkman's defense and, 184, 185

Kronstadt sailors (*cont.*)
strike of, 210-211
Kropotkin, Peter, 106
collectivity and, 58
followers of, 74
Mother Earth and, 136
sexual freedom and, 162-163
violence and, 60-61
Ku Klux Klan, World War I and, 189

labor movement, 75
Haymarket Affair and, 41-42
women's strikes and, 75
Ladies' Home Journal, on women's role, 167
"law and order" government, anarchism versus, 51-53
Lawrence, Mass., textile strike, 38
Lazarus, Emma, 34
libertarian, Emma Goldman as, 139
libertarianism, definition of, 50
Liberty Bonds, 189
Lincoln, Abraham, 119
Living My Life (Emma Goldman), 218
love, 168

love (*cont.*)
  women's oppression and, 161-163
Lower East Side (New York):
  description of, 65
  Emma Goldman on, 64
loyalty oaths, Red Scare and, 200

McKinley, William, 137
  assassination of, 118-121, 123-127, 195
Malatesta, Enrico, 106
Malcolm X, 102
Mann, Thomas, 221
Mannin, Ethel, 232
Manning, Henry, Cardinal, 95
marriage:
  in Barcelona, 226
  Emma Goldman's to Jim Colton, 216-217
  Emma Goldman's to Jacob Kershner, 40-41
  Emma Goldman's views on, 32-33, 72, 96, 160-162
Marx, Karl, 56-57
May Day (1891), 75
  bomb mailing on, 190
Mayflower, 188
Memoirs (Alexander Berkman), 84

Mencken, H. L., 118
Michel, Louise, 106
midwifery, 106, 107, 168
militias, Spanish, 228
Miller, Herman, 111
Minkin, Anna, 66, 68, 70-71, 75
Minkin, Helen, 66, 68, 70-72
Missouri State Prison, 193
Modern School, closing of, 200
Mooney, Thomas, 190
  fight for life of, 177-178, 185-186
Mooney-Billings Defense Committee, 178, 184-185
Morality, New, 131
Morgan, J. P., 190
Most, John, 45, 65, 66, 93
  description of, 67-68
  Emma Goldman and, 69-75, 88-89, 103
  H. C. Frick assassination attempt and, 87-88
  women and, 70-74
Mother Earth, 134-136, 150
  alien expulsion and, 192
  Alexander Berkman and, 139
  contribution of, 136
  Emma Goldman's deportation and, 195

Mother Earth (cont.)
  Paul Orleneff and, 134-135
  raid on, 181
  suppression of, 165
Murray, Robert K., 192
Mussolini, Benito, 218
Mutual Aid (Peter Kropotkin), 58
My Disillusionment in Russia (Emma Goldman), 215

Nationalism, New, 131
Nazi Party (German), 218
Neiman, Fred, *see* Czolgosz, Leon
Neo-Malthusian Congress, birth control and, 113, 169
New Criticism, 131
New Deal, 220
New Democracy, 131
New Drama, 131, 132
  Russian, 133
New Freedom, 131
"new literature," 106
New Nationalism, 131
New Painting, 131
New Poetry, 131
New Psychology, 132
New Republic, 131
New Theology, 131

New York *World,* 96
Nietzsche, Friedrich, 106
nobles, Russian, 3
No-Conscription League, 179-184
No-Conscription Manifesto, 181
nurse, Emma Goldman as, 101-102

organizer, Emma Goldman as, 140, 168
Orleneff, Paul, 133-135
Orwell, George, 224, 228

pacifists, 174-175
  antidraft movement and, 179-184
  maltreatment of, 189
Painting, New, 131
Palmer, A. Mitchell, 190, 191, 196-197
Pan-American Exposition, 118-120
Panic of 1893, 93-95
Paris Exposition (1900), 111-112, 118
"patriotic" societies, 189
patriotism:
  perverted, 155
  World War I and, 188-189

peasants, 3, 8-9

Pennsylvania coal miners, strike of, 128

People's Army, Spanish, 229

Petrushka (a stable boy), 9-11

Pinkerton detectives:
Haymarket Affair and, 42
Homestead strike and, 79, 80

Poetry, New, 131

pogroms, 5, 25, 128

police, collusion with vigilantes by, 154

police harassment, 95-96, 138, 147-148
antidraft movement and, 180
Defense Committee rally and, 185
depression of 1908 and, 144-145

political assassination, 27, 115-117
attempted, 77, 81-88, 115
of William McKinley, 120-127
of other presidents, 119

Popular Front government, Spanish, 229, 231

populism (Russian):
aims of, 23, 26-28

populism (cont.)
czarist reaction to, 24

pregnancy:
birth control and, 168-171
women's oppression and, 160

Preparedness Parade bombing, 175-177

"Preparedness—the Road to Universal Slaughter" (Emma Goldman), 176

press, the, 96-97, 108

Preston-Longley, Sarah, 12

prisons:
in Barcelona, 226
in Bolshevik Russia, 205
Emma Goldman in, 99-103, 193-194

progress, spirit of, 130-131

"propaganda by deed," 59, 115-117
Alexander Berkman's, 81-87

property, communal ownership of, 56-57

prostitution, 82-83, 85-86
in Barcelona, 226
in Bolshevik Russia, 205-206
women's oppression and, 165

Proudhon, Pierre-Joseph, 53-54, 112

"Psychology of Political Violence, The" (Emma Goldman), 116
public speaking, Emma Goldman's, 71, 73-74, 107-110
on birth control, 168-171
in Union Square, 94-95
Puritanism, women's oppression and, 164-165

radical, definition of, 23
radicals:
aims of, 23, 26-27
government reaction to, 23-24, 60
Palmer raids and, 196-197
persecution of, 125-128
witch hunt against, 189, 200
rallies, antidraft, 179-180
Rebel in Paradise (Richard Drinnon), 194
Red Ark, *see Buford, U.S.S.*
Red Cross, 189
Red Scare, 188-202
Reitman, Dr. Ben L.:
background of, 148-149
Emma Goldman and, 145-151, 153-159, 170
description of, 146
as Hobo King, 145-146, 149

Reitman (*cont.*)
vigilante torture of, 154-155
relief, Panic of 1893 and, 93-94
religion:
anarchists and, 96
Emma Goldman's, 17
Republicans, Spanish Civil War and, 225, 229
revolution:
anarchism and, 59-60
Bolshevik betrayal of, 205-213
Spanish anarchist, 225-229
violence and, 59-61
revolutionaries, St. Petersburg, 26-28
Rockefeller, John D., 190
Roosevelt, Franklin D., 191, 220
Roosevelt, Theodore:
anti-anarchism of, 126
William Buwalda and, 151
New Era and, 130-131
on women's role, 167
Russell, Bertrand, 215, 221
Russia, 217
anarchists in, 49, 209, 210, 212
anti-Semitism in, 4-5, 128

Russia (*cont.*)
exiled actors of, 132-133
Emma Goldman and, 1-11, 204-213
populism in, 23-24, 26-28
Spanish Civil War and, 231
Russian Revolution (1917), 177, 186
betrayal of, 205-213
early triumph of, 186
public defense of, 196

Sachs's Café, 65-66, 71
San Diego *Tribune,* 152-153
San Francisco Law and Order Committee, 175
Sasha, *see* Berkman, Alexander
Saturday Evening Post, 188
self-determination, populism and, 23
Serge, Victor, 203
serfs, Russian, 3
sewing, as Emma Goldman's livelihood, 62, 64, 70-72
sex, 106, 108, 109
women's oppression and, 161-165
sexual freedom, 161-163
Emma Goldman and, 112

Shaw, George Bernard, 132
Smith, E. G., as Emma Goldman's alias, 132
smoking, Emma Goldman's public, 168
smugglers, Russian border, 21-22
social idealism:
communal ownership of wealth and, 56-57
definition of, 50
socialism, 192
anarchism and, 56-58
Emma Goldman and, 39-40
Spanish Civil War and, 225
social privilege, versus anarchism, 58
social revolution, Spain and, 225-229
Social Significance of the Modern Drama, The (Emma Goldman), 132
Solotaroff (an anarchist), 64, 65
Spain:
anarchists in, 49
Civil War in, 223-233
State, the (*see also* government):
anarchist view of, 96
power of, 194

Steffens, Lincoln, 90, 212-213
Stella Cominsky, 132, 133, 222
Stone, Carl, 111, 113
strikes, 59
    as "communist plot," 190
    Homestead, 78-81
    women's, 75
Strindberg, August, 132
students, radical activities of Russian, 26-27
suffragists, 165-167
    futility of, 172-173

terrorism (*see also* assassination; violence), 97
textbooks, Red Scare and, 200
Theology, New, 131
Thoreau, Henry David, 49
Trepov, General, shooting of (1878), 27
trials, 90-92, 170-171, 181-184
Trotsky, Leon, 210
Turner, John, 128-129
Twain, Mark, 144

unemployment:
    Barcelona and, 227
    Depression of 1908 and, 144

unemployment (*cont.*)
    Panic of 1893 and, 93-94
unions, 75
    Homestead strike and, 79
    International Workers of the World, 146
United Jewish Charities of Rochester, 37
United States:
    "equality" myth of, 38-39
    factory work in, 36-39
    immigrants in, 35-39

vigilante committees, 152-157
violence (*see also* assassination):
    conspiracy trial and, 183
    Emma Goldman's evaluation of, 115-117
    revolution and, 59-61
    vigilante, 152-153, 197
vote, the, 166
    futility of, 59, 172-173
    women and, 132, 165-167, 172-173

wage discrimination, women and, 173
Wagner, Richard, 106
Waldheim Cemetery (Chicago), 235

wealth:
  communal ownership of, 56-57
  unequal distribution of, 49-50
West, Rebecca, 104
White, Dr., at Blackwell's Island Penitentiary, 101-102
Wilson, Woodrow:
  Thomas Mooney's execution and, 178, 185-186
  Red Scare and, 199
  World War I and, 179
woman question, the, 158-173
women:
  in Barcelona, 226
  Jewish, 159-160
  job discrimination and, 94
  labor strikes of, 75
  liberated, 161
  Most's view of, 70, 74
  New, 131-132
  stereotype for, 167
women's oppression, 160-161

women's oppression (cont.)
  Emma Goldman and, 18, 41, 171-173
  International Anarchist Congress and, 112
  love and, 161-163
  Mother Earth and, 136
  marriage and, 160-162
  pregnancy and, 160, 168-171
  root of, 171-172
  sex and, 161-165
women's suffrage, 132, 166, 172-173
Woodcock, George, 228
workers, exploitation of, 36-39
World War I:
  American involvement in, 174-175
  antidraft movement and, 179-184
  Bolshevik withdrawal from, 189
  hysteria during, 188-189

Zasulich, Vera, 27-28, 161

ABOUT THE AUTHOR

The new feminists hope to restore women to history. In this spirit, Alix Shulman chose to write about Emma Goldman, one of America's most influential radicals, whose life story was for a long time almost erased from our history books.

Alix Shulman was born and grew up in Cleveland, Ohio, and was graduated from Western Reserve University there. Later she studied philosophy at Columbia and mathematics at New York University. In addition to this biography, Mrs. Shulman has edited a collection of Emma Goldman's papers, and she has written several stories for young readers.

With her husband and two children she now lives in New York City. She is active in the feminist movement and especially concerned with the portrayal of women in children's literature.